Dealing Creatively with Death

i

Ernest Morgan

DEALING

CREATIVELY

WITH DEATH

A Manual of Death Education
and Simple Burial

by Ernest Morgan

edited by Jenifer Morgan

Barclay House
35-19 215 Place
Bayside, New York 11361

Permission to Reprint: Persons wishing to reprint a paragraph or two of material which is original to this book may do so if credit is given. Longer reprints by nonprofit groups, not to exceed five pages, are welcomed if the following credit line is used: "from *Dealing Creatively with Death: A Manual of Death Education and Simple Burial,* by Ernest Morgan, edited by Jenifer Morgan, and published by Barclay House, 35-19 215 Place, Bayside, N.Y. 11361." We would appreciate it if you send us a copy of the publication you use our material in, or at least notify us of its use. For any other use of our material, please contact Barclay House Permissions Dept.

Composition by Celo Book Production Service, 346 Seven Mile Ridge Road, Burnsville, North Carolina 28714.

Library of Congress Cataloging-in-Publication Data

Morgan, Ernest.
    Dealing creatively with death: a manual of death education and simple
  burial / by Ernest Morgan; edited by Jenifer Morgan.—12th rev. ed.
    p. cm.
  Includes bibliographical references and index.
  ISBN 0-935016-79-1 : $11.95
  1. Death—Handbooks, manuals, etc.. 2. Burial—Handbooks,
  etc. 3. Funeral rites and ceremonies—Handbooks, manuals,
  etc. I. Morgan, Jenifer. II. Title.
  BD444.M658 1990
  306.9—dc20
                             90-20830
                             CIP

Poems 40 (p.144), 46 and 49 (pages 139-140) are reprinted with permission of Macmillan Publishing Company from *Fruit-Gathering* by Rabindranath Tagore. Copyright © 1916 by Macmillan Publishing Co., Inc., renewed 1944 by Rabindranath Tagore.

Poems 84, 87 and 90 (pages 138-139) are reprinted with permission of Macmillan Publishing Company from *Gitanjali,* by Rabindranath Tagore, Copyright © 1916 by Macmillan Publishing Company.

TABLE OF CONTENTS

INTRODUCTION TO THE TWELFTH EDITION

Important changes have occurred in the fields of death and dying since the eleventh edition of the *Manual* was published in 1988, and the cost of funerals continues to rise. Despite consumer protection efforts, these costs have increased much more rapidly than the consumer price index. This edition offers new information for coping with this problem, and solid counsel in dealing with pre-need sales, which have been rapidly increasing.

The highly publicized AIDS epidemic strongly affects the process of bereavement, care for the dying, and arrangements for disposition of the body. This is dealt with in Chapter 3, "Bereavement;" Chapter 2, "Living with Dying;" and Chapter 5, "Simple Burial and Cremation." References for further information are given.

The shocking increase in youth suicide is discussed in Chapter 4, "The Right to Die," looking briefly at causes and offering suggestions for prevention and further study.

Less well known is the rapid increase in the number of organ transplants performed. For example, in 1982 there were 103 heart transplants in the U.S. In 1988 that number had increased to 1,647. In the same year, we are told, there were 450,000 bone grafts. New networks have developed to coordinate organ donations in both the United States and Canada, and new laws have been passed providing guidelines. These changes, and the sharply increased need for organ donations, are discussed in Chapter 8, "How the Dead Can Help the Living," and Appendix 8, "Anatomical Gifts."

A quiet revolution is taking place in hospice care. The number of hospices in the National Hospice Organization has tripled since 1984. Chapter 2, "Living with Dying," reflects the changes taking place, including use of hospice care for patients with Alzheimer's Disease.

Chapter 3, "Bereavement," has been substantially rewritten to reflect our growing understanding of grieving, and the growth potential which it contains.

Rapid changes in law are taking place in response to the medical ability to prolong life in the dying, and the growing struggle, as a result, to avoid needless suffering and expense. Latest information on the rights of patients and families, and how to implement these rights, is contained in Chapter 4, "The Right to Die," and appendix 4, "Living Will."

As with each previous edition for the past 28 years, the book has been massively revised, developing gradually into a small encyclopedia combining time tested wisdom with timely relevance. We are grateful for the suggestions of our readers and invite them to send us criticisms and information which may be useful in future editions.

FOREWORD

Of the many people who helped me over the years with writing projects, I count Ernest Morgan as *primus inter pares* — first among equals.

In the early 1960s, when I was preparing *The American Way of Death*, I ran across his *Manual of Simple Burial* — a brilliant little volume of advice to the hapless survivor who wants to avoid the full-fig funeral, with all the costly trimmings, decreed by the undertakers as what they are pleased to call "the standard American funeral."

Once, years ago, Ernest Morgan and I shared a flight from Seattle to Oakland. In the course of our conversation I asked what motivated him to continue active in the field of Death Education and Simple Burial. He looked out the window for a while, then he said, "There are three reasons. First, working in this field is contributing to my own emotional maturity — my acceptance of death, my appreciation of life and my concern for my fellow beings.

"Second, I desire social change and a more humane and cooperative society. At no time are people more prone to think about life values, and more open to change, than at a time of death, or in thinking about death. This is a strategic time to influence them creatively, and combat what is phony, exploitative and ostentatious in American life.

"Third, the *Manual* is making money for the Arthur Morgan School!"

Mr. Morgan and I became firm penpals and have corresponded for two decades. He was immeasurably helpful in giving guidance and practical advice when I was writing *The American Way of Death*, and for years thereafter as we fought in our respective communities what one writer called "the battle of the Bier Barons."

Unlike the *Manual*, my own book does not deal with philosophic approaches to death and dying, but with the funeral industry. In his review of *The American Way of Death*, Evelyn Waugh wrote that "the trouble with Miss Mitford is that she has no stated attitude towards death." I wrote my sister Nancy, who was a friend of Waugh's, "Tell Evelyn that I *do* have an attitude towards death. I'm against it." (When

I told Ernest Morgan this, he commented in his wry, dry fashion, "Better not abolish death. If we do, people will need a government permit to have a baby!")

In contrast with earlier editions of the *Manual*, this expanded version, while retaining its useful information about
memorial societies, bequeathal of remains to medical schools, etc., goes more deeply into the practical and philosophical concerns of death and dying.

His perceptive, humane views on these matters should provide great solace to the terminally ill and their families.

—Jessica Mitford

PREFACE / *How this Book Happened*

My father, Arthur E. Morgan, was an intensely creative man whose activities had a lasting impact in several areas of American life. He had long felt that American funeral practices could be simpler and more meaningful. In 1948, he formed the Burial Committee of the Yellow Springs Meeting (Quaker) to study the matter in a systematic way.

After five years of study his committee evolved a plan whereby the Meeting would care for its own dead, handling the paper work, building the boxes, conveying the bodies to a crematory and arranging memorial services — all without professional assistance.

In 1953 I was drafted by the Meeting to chair this committee. I had no special interest in the project but did not wish to avoid responsibility, so I accepted. After all, I thought, I am a grown man, I can probably handle a dead body as well as the next fellow.

During the five years of study no one in the Meeting had died, but as soon as I became chairman they started dying! Then I discovered that what I had anticipated to be a disagreeable chore turned out to be a meaningful privilege — serving one's friends at a time of profound need. The plan worked well at small cost, and the memorial services became a comfort and an inspiration to all concerned.

Then, quite by accident, our little Burial Committee got nationwide publicity. Letters poured in, asking for information. Gosh, I thought, I can't answer all these letters, I'll mimeograph a few sheets to send these people. Then another thought occurred to me. A burial committee is fine for a close-knit rural group like ours, but in most situations a memorial society which works with funeral directors is more practical. I'd better include some information on memorial societies. So I started digging out this information. (There was no memorial society association then.)

A short time later, my stepmother, Lucy Morgan, asked me to make arrangements for her to leave her body to the University Medical School. She was a thrifty soul. "I don't want my body wasted," she said. So I went and met Dr. Graves (!) who was dean of the anatomy department. Dr. Graves was (almost too) enthusiastic. "If only more people would do this! There's a serious shortage of bodies in many areas." So I saw that I'd better tell people about leaving their bodies to a medical school.

Another five years passed. Instead of a few sheets I had a 64-page book, *A Manual of Simple Burial.* It appeared in 1962, printed by Celo Press, a division of the Arthur Morgan School which my wife and I were launching then. It was well received.

In 1963, another surprise. The Co-op League called a meeting to federate the memorial societies of the U.S. and Canada. Would I be a keynote speaker? I seemed to have become an authority. Soon I was on the Board of the Continental Association of Funeral and Memorial Societies. Who was it said, "There is a destiny that shapes our ends..."?

The book sold well and helped support the school. New editions followed, each extensively revised. Howard Raether, then Executive Director of the National Funeral Directors Association, once asked me, "How come you change the book so much between editions?" All I could say was, "Times change, and new ideas and information keep coming."

One thing I learned was that people turn their backs on the idea of death and are thus inhibited from joining a memorial society or planning ahead. Death education is almost a prerequisite for coming to grips with the question. So with our sixth edition we changed the title to *A Manual of Death Education and Simple Burial.* Sales continued to grow.

In 1971 my wife died of cancer after a long illness. During her final months we kept her at home where her life could be filled with love and fellowship and music—our introduction to what we now call hospice. Another dimension was thus added to the *Manual.*

Looking back, I realize that much of the book came from my long life in a warm, cohesive family where death was a repeated visitor, and from half a century in a small community where life and death were deeply shared. That was my university, which was supplemented by reading and by association with many knowledgeable people.

No one has benefited more from reading this book than I have from writing it. As a child I was devoted to my father, a man of great strength and gentleness. Accepting his death was hard for me and writing this *Manual* made it possible for me to face reality and accept his death and that of others whom I loved.

The *Manual* (now titled *Dealing Creatively with Death*) is no longer my book but belongs as well to a host of friends and scholars who have helped with it. In particular, my daughter Jenifer has done much of the research and writing for recent editions and has been my most faithful and exacting critic. Now in my eighty-sixth year I hope she will have a hand in future editions and will carry it on when I am gone.

Proceeds from the book still go to the Arthur Morgan school, and an alumnus of the school, David Zinn, has taken over the publishing through his firm, Barclay House Books.

—*Ernest Morgan*

INTRODUCTION / *About Accepting Death*

If we were to walk across the fields in summertime to some undisturbed spot and mark off a piece of ground say four feet square and then examine this little area minutely, we would find an astonishing variety of life. There would be many species of plants; possibly a mouse's nest, and other small creatures. Then, resorting to a microscope, we would observe an incredible host of microorganisms functioning in association with the larger life forms. But we would not stop there. We would start digging, exploring for additional life underground. There, too, we would find insects, nematodes, earthworms of various kinds, and a fresh array of bacteria. Nor would we necessarily stop when we reached bedrock. If that rock happened to be Ohio limestone there would be several hundred feet of dense fossil deposits laid down through millions of years, representing myriad species and astronomical numbers of individual lives.

In that little square of ground we would have seen an interdependent community of life in which birth and death were continuously taking place and in which diverse life forms were sheltering and nourishing one another. Written in the rocks beneath was a story of a similar process going back through eons of time.

Humankind is part of the ongoing community of nature, on a world scale, subject to the same cycle of birth and death which governs all other creatures and, like them, totally dependent on other life. Sometimes, in our high-rise apartments, our manicured suburbs and our chromium plated institutions we tend to forget this.

Our need is not to conquer nature but to live in harmony with it. This does not mean rejecting our technology, but it does mean controlling our numbers, quieting our egos, and simplifying our lifestyles.

Birth and death are as natural for us as for the myriad creatures in that little square of ground. When we have learned to accept ourselves as part of the community of nature, then we can accept death as part of the natural order of things.

We commonly act as if we, and those we love, were going to live forever. But we are wrong, for all must die—nor can we know when this will happen.

In our culture we tend to avoid the subject of death. This is unfortunate, for death is a normal and necessary part of life. Until we learn to face it honestly and accept it, we are not living at our best.

If we are to appreciate our fellows, if we are to live with patience, gentleness and love, let us be about it today, for life is short.

1 DEATH EDUCATION

This chapter has three functions.
First is to break the ice—for those who need to have it broken—and help people think and talk about death more easily. Until they are able to do this without feeling uncomfortable they will have difficulty in benefiting from the ensuing chapters.
Second is to review briefly the emergence of death education and to discuss some of the ways in which it is strongly relevant to life, both of the individual and of society.
Third, this chapter gives a brief overview of the rest of the book, suggesting possible uses of the remaining chapters, and offering suggestions for persons who may be leading classes or discussions on the topic.

Why Death Education?

Death education is for everyone, because it relates not just to death but to our feelings about ourselves and nature and the universe we live in. A prime function of death education is to help us to think and feel deeply about the meaning of life in its many relationships—to help mature our values. As Abraham Maslow wrote, after recovering from a heart attack, "The confrontation with death—and the reprieve from it—makes everything look so precious, so sacred, so beautiful that I feel more strongly than ever the impulse to live it, to embrace it and to let myself be overwhelmed by it."[1] Confronting death imaginatively through experience, reading, thinking, lectures and discussions often has the paradoxical effect of enriching life.

As we pass beyond the fear and avoidance of death so common in our culture, we can learn to accept dying as an appropriate culmination of life. To do this we need to be able to talk freely with our loved ones about death—both our own and theirs, whether imminent or remote.

Death education does not avoid grief—and should not if it could—but it can help us to cope with grief in a creative way so that we may grow in the quality of our lives. It can help us also to relate meaningfully to dying persons, and to meet the social and emotional needs of the survivors—including ourselves.

1

Then, too, it can help us deal wisely with practical matters that must be faced at time of death, thus avoiding unnecessary ostentation, suffering and expense.

Death education is doubly valuable for those whose work brings them into frequent contact with dying, death and/or bereavement. These include not only health professionals, counsellors and clergy, but also law enforcement, military and disaster personnel who work with survivors of major loss and sudden death.

The Growth of Death Education

Forty years ago the subject of death was taboo in polite society, as sex had been in earlier days. In 1959, Dr. LeRoy Bowman's sociological study, *The American Funeral*, and Herman Feifel's *The Meaning of Death* cracked the barrier. In 1962 the first edition of my *Manual* appeared, followed in 1963 by Ruth Harmer's *The High Cost of Dying* and Jessica Mitford's bombshell, *The American Way of Death*. That same year the memorial societies emerged, largely under church leadership, as a united, continent-wide movement.

In 1967 Earl Grollman's *Explaining Death to Children* was published, and in 1969 Elisabeth Kubler-Ross gave the movement fresh depth and impetus with her classic *On Death and Dying*, stressing the need for death education among health care professionals. Since that time, hundreds of books and thousands of articles have appeared.

In 1975, the Forum (now Association) for Death Education and Counseling was organized, giving form and substance to the movement, and grew to over one thousand members working professionally in the field. Thousands of schools and colleges have classes in death education. Many churches likewise conduct seminars and conferences on the subject. Important, too, it has become a significant topic in courses in sociology, psychology, health care disciplines, literature, law, art, biology, philosophy, religion, and consumer education.

Simultaneously, hospice programs began in the United States. The National Hospice Organization was formed in 1977 to provide national leadership in education, research, standard setting and advocacy. Hospices now train thousands of volunteers and professionals to deal humanely with dying and death. See Chapter 2, "Living With Dying."

Clearly, death education has come into its own.

About the Death Educator

Educators and counselors need to have a deep understanding and acceptance of death and dying. It is this understanding, combined with personal experience, which qualifies one to teach. It is the ability to share this experience and understanding directly from the heart that makes a fine teacher.

Similarly, an important qualification — perhaps the most important qualification — for anyone to counsel bereaved persons is that the counselor has dealt creatively with suffering and is able to reach out to, and empathize with, the person being counseled. Most such counselors — at least the good ones — have been drawn into the field by virtue of their own experience and what they have learned from it.

Such counseling, at its best, is a two-way experience in which the counselor as well as the counseled experiences growth. That is one of the rewards of being a counselor.

In recent years, arrangements have been made for the certification of counsellors in this field, by the Association for Death Education and Counselling. See Appendix 2, "Organizations" for listing. But this does not remove the responsibility of the rest of us to assist in this area when occasion arises.

Death Education for Children

Children have more awareness of death than most of us realize. Fairy tales, movies and television programs abound in death, as does the world of nature which they see about them.

Herman Feifel comments that "The shaping impact of awareness of death is active at all levels."[2] By age two, children's play demonstrates an awareness of death. Children three to five years of age commonly see death as temporary and reversible. From about five to nine years of age the finality is recognized and children begin to understand that death is an inevitable part of life. At first they think of it as something that happens to others, but not to themselves; later they realize it will someday happen to them. By age ten, if not before, most children understand the reality of death as adults do.[3]

Acceptance of death as part of life needs to be incorporated into a child's normal activities at home and at school. On occasions of deaths in my own family, the children were kept close to the center of family life and given roles to carry out in family activities relating to the deaths. This gave comfort to the adults as well as to the children.

Although wildly emotional outbursts may be upsetting to children, adults should not try to conceal their emotions from their children. Naturalness and honesty are basic. The physical fact of death should be explained and children should not be discouraged from touching dead things if they wish. It should be explained that dead things feel no pain, as children commonly have great fear of pain. It helps to explain that we are part of the world of nature and share with all other creatures the cycle of life and death. For each of us there is a time to be born, to grow and flourish, and then to die. Fears are lessened if the emphasis is on the beauty of life.

The Challenge of Man-Made Death

A major challenge to death education—and one of its greatest potentials for usefulness, is in confronting the issues of man-made death. The first of these—now happily diminishing (in 1990) is the threat of nuclear war. The nations of the world do, however, own nuclear weapons with explosive power equal to fifteen thousand million tons of TNT, and these weapons are proliferating. The other wing of the nuclear threat is pollution, as millions of tons of radioactive waste, with a half-life of thousands of years, pile up from the manufacture of nuclear weapons and from the generating of nuclear power.

A second threat, as dangerous and difficult as the nuclear one, is the environmental crisis. During the current half-century the world will have lost half its arable land to erosion and desertification, and will have nearly trebled its human population. Each second of the day and night we are losing an acre of forest and adding three people to the population. The greenhouse effect is starting, the ozone layer is thinning, the pollution of air and water is rising and the ocean phytoplankton, which produce two-thirds of the world's oxygen, is diminishing. Our present course, if unchanged, can lead to suffering and death beyond anything experienced in human history.

Death education can help us to confront and deal with both the threats of war and the crisis of the environment. It can help us also to cope with the tendency to despair. Commenting on the nuclear menace, sociologist Henrik Infield exclaimed, "If we're going to be blown up, let's be blown up doing something worthwhile!" In other words, we should accept the reality of the dangers that face us, then place our bets on life!

There are constructive ways in which we can deal with the prospect of human extinction. To take a hand in our own destiny, even on a tiny scale, improves our chances and, besides, gives us a sense of empowerment which is essential to our emotional well-being.

A teacher in Seattle once asked her students: "How many of you think there might be a nuclear war?" Hands were raised by every child but one. "And you, Sally, why aren't you expecting that?"

"Well, Mommy and Daddy are working for disarmament and I think they're going to win."

Human solidarity is important. For an old-timer like myself, there is a temptation to take refuge in the thought that I'm likely to be dead and gone before hell breaks loose. But I quickly reject this impulse as cowardly and take my stand with the young people who will inherit the future. We can't avoid our individual deaths, but we can try, by thoughtful and concerted action, to avoid the death of our civilization. This idea can give us inspiration and hope.

Other Man-Made Deaths

War and ecological disaster are not the only forms of man-made death that need to be dealt with openly. There are difficult social questions, such as capital punishment, abortion, euthanasia, accidental deaths and suicide. Some of these issues are beyond the scope of this book, but euthanasia and suicide are dealt with at length in Chapter 4, "The Right to Die."

Life After Death

The continuity of biological life is obvious. Also evident is the continuity of cultural patterns and values. The continuity of the individual soul is an article of faith with most major religions of the world. Christianity, Judaism and Islam hold the view that the soul maintains its ego/individuality throughout eternity. In the East, Hinduism and Buddhism generally stress a series of reincarnations in different egos eventually leading to merging of the individual soul (Atman) into the cosmic soul (Brahman, or Nirvana).

The existence and nature of an afterlife has been inferred from presumed interactions with spirits of the dead (mediums, apparitions, spirit photographs and recordings, and possession, for example), and from apparently confirmed memories of previous incarnations. Recently much attention has been given to evidence derived from "near death experiences" of people at or near death who revived. Elisabeth Kubler-Ross says she has spoken to more than 1,000 such people, and Raymond Moody's *Life After Life* describes several such experiences in detail.

Some researchers emphasize the lack of conclusive proof for religious dogmas, and for the theory that life after death explains these phenomena. Others suggest that the idea of an afterlife explains the various phenomena more readily than do other theories. While ideas about an afterlife are many and varied, most hold that death is a transition to a new state of being; and that the quality of that state depends at least in part on how we lived on earth and the state of our spiritual development. References for further study are included in Appendix 1, "Bibliography."

How to Go About Death Education

First of all, consider the makeup and needs of the class. How old are the students? Is it made up of hospice volunteers who need to relate to dying persons? Is it a group of health professionals and, if so, at what level? Is it an adult seminar including people with problems of grief and loss? Is it for church people considering plans for their own last rites and arrangements, or perhaps planning a support group for assisting bereaved families?

This has a bearing on the topics to be included and what emphasis to give to each. Teachers need to be sensitive to the particular needs they are dealing with and the feelings that may be evoked. It helps to circulate a questionnaire to the members of the class at the outset, including such questions as: "Why are you taking this course?", "What was your most significant experience with death?", "Do you have any special death-related experiences which you bring to the class?"

In all class discussions and role playing, participation should be voluntary and students should not be pressed for answers. Offering alternative assignments can allow students to decide whether or not to approach an emotionally difficult subject. Books containing teaching resources are listed in Appendix 1.

Application of the Remaining Chapters

Each chapter of this Manual presents a topic or topics that may be included in a syllabus.

"Living with Dying," Chapter 2, stressing home care for the terminally ill, will be of special interest to hospice workers and other health care personnel. Churches may use it to help in supporting home care for parishioners. Memorial Society members and others will be interested in planning to meet their families' needs. Family life courses will also find this material helpful.

"Bereavement," Chapter 3, is an essential topic for all of us, as experience of loss is universal. Hospice workers are committed to bereavement support. Every counselor, clergyman and health care worker needs the information this chapter provides. Churches will find it helpful in encouraging congregational support of the bereaved in the church community.

"The Right to Die," Chapter 4, is of special interest to persons facing terminal illness within their families and to those who wish to make provision in advance to assure that they will have some control over their own deaths. Likewise it is of interest to all persons involved in health care, including, of course, hospice workers. Students of law and philosophy also will find this frequently controversial presentation interesting. This chapter deals also with the increasingly urgent problem of suicide and the role of the teacher in dealing with this problem.

"Simple Burial and Cremation," Chapter 5, presents the philosophy and practice of planning for and handling a death in the family in a simple manner—information every family should have. Professionals and volunteers who work with the dying can be of great service in making this information available. Church leaders, too, will want this information to meet the needs of their religious communities. As with memorial societies, this topic should be included in consumer education.

"Memorial Societies," Chapter 6, should be understood by all who work with death and dying—or who expect to die someday! They have a unique role in assisting families who desire simplicity and economy in funeral arrangements.

"Death Ceremonies," Chapter 7, are very important in meeting the social and emotional needs of survivors at a time of death. This chapter has been included at the request of several readers who felt that alternative types of ceremonies would better meet these needs. It is also useful to church people and others who may be concerned with planning a service. Special attention is given to memorial services.

"How the Dead Can Help the Living," Chapter 8, encourages people to make anatomical gifts at the time of death, and tells how to plan accordingly. This is an urgent concern at the present time, of special relevance to health professionals, biologists and lawyers.

Extensive material, including a selected bibliography on death education, has been assembled in the appendices at the back of this book, where it will be updated with each new reprint.

REFERENCES

[1]From a letter to Dr. Rollo May, as it appeared in *Love and Will*, by Rollo May. W.W. Norton, 1969. Used with permission.

[2]Herman Feifel, "The Meaning of Death in American Society," in *Death Education*, by Donald Irish and Betty Green. Cambridge, MA: Schenkman Publishing Company, 1971, p. 5.

[3]De Spelder & Strickland, *The Last Dance: Encountering Death & Dying*, Palo Alto, CA: Mayfield Publishing Co., 1983. Includes a good summary of developmental studies of children's concepts of death.

2 LIVING WITH DYING

In this chapter I tell of my experience in caring for a dying patient at home and discuss how to relate to a dying person in a positive way. Also discussed are group support for the family of a dying person and how to relate to a dying child. These things are described as part of the hospice concept and the growing hospice movement. Appendix 4 reviews financial help available for home care. I am indebted to friends in the Hospice movement, especially Donna O'Toole, of Rainbow Connections, for help with this chapter.

A Personal Experience in Home Care

I had never heard of the hospice philosophy in 1971 when my wife, Elizabeth, was dying of cancer, but my daughter and I had the basic concept. It was Elizabeth's wish to spend her last weeks at home, so we brought her there.

Arrangements were not complicated. My daughter got instructions at the hospital and then passed them along to me — how to give shots, change bedding, give baths and take care of toilet needs. How to take pulse and temperature we already knew, and keeping a hospital chart was a simple routine. We borrowed a hospital bed, an over-bed table, and a commode chair, and contrived a stand for the intravenous fluids from a sturdy music rack. Such incidentals as a rubber sheet and bedpan were purchased or borrowed. When intravenous medication was prescribed, a nurse from the health department came and started it. All in all, it wasn't as difficult as we had expected and was easier because we loved the patient. The chief requirement was the desire and willingness to do it.

We had a good working relationship with the doctor, who talked on the phone with us every couple of days, made medical decisions, and prescribed medicines. Elizabeth experienced chronic pain, controlled by shots whenever she called for them, as instructed by the doctor. At that time there was no hospice organization, but we had strong community support. Friends ran errands and did shopping for us and gave a hand wherever needed.

9

The best part about home care was that my wife was surrounded by loving family members and friends. She loved music and was a fine musician, so by her bed we put an FM radio that brought in several National Public Radio stations. (Bless NPR!) She tried to have a visit with each of her students before she died, and family and friends from far and near came to see her. Some sang for her—folk songs and gospel hymns. Often they embraced her. It was a warmly human situation.

Elizabeth's acceptance of death was helped by turning much of her attention outside herself. As her strength permitted, she talked with the young people she knew, discussing their problems and plans. I recall an evening at the hospital, before she came home. Talking with the doctor, she said, "There's a little girl at school to whom I've promised the lead in next year's operetta, and she needs it so badly! I've just got to have another year." The doctor had tears in his eyes when he left the room, and he put her back on chemotherapy for one more try.

Elizabeth accepted the prospect of death calmly, almost cheerfully, but fought hard for life. We prepared "green drinks" and other things said to cause remissions, and none of us gave up hope until the very end. We knew that she was going to die, however, and talked about it frankly. Elizabeth told me shortly before she died how much it meant to her that we were able to accept her death. Some dying persons whose families would not accept their death or talk about it have written me, a stranger, to fill this void. Her actual death was peaceful, as she quietly stopped breathing.

Elizabeth had been afraid her death might upset the students at the Arthur Morgan School, with whom she had a very close relationship. Accordingly we prepared together a talk which I gave them, discussing life and death. They received it thoughtfully and seemed to benefit from it. One of these students, a few years later, died of bone cancer following the amputation of both legs. The family's psychologist told me afterwards that the buoyant and understanding spirit he maintained directly reflected his experience of Elizabeth Morgan's death.

My Daughter Jenifer's Comments

"When we realized in 1971 that Mother was losing her two-year battle with cancer, I was glad to be able to bring my two children, then ten and twelve years old, and help take care of her. Dad bought an old house trailer and set it up for us nearby, and I went to the hospital and learned general practical nursing.

"We shared the general housework and physical care of Mother, while I did most of the cooking and each evening gave her a backrub, which seemed to be especially comforting. I had time to go out occasionally with friends and participate in a peer counseling support group. Through this, one friend learned of the struggle I was having caring for one of my children, whose personality clashed with Mother's, and she invited him to stay with her family for awhile. That helped a lot, though often I felt torn in the evenings between spending time with the children or giving the special care that would ease Mother's nights.

"Cooking presented its own problems. Mother's tastes and needs were simple—she especially loved lamb chops and baked custard—but one effect of the cancer was to upset the digestive system so that nothing really tasted good or digested easily. Thus I found myself feeling inadequate in caring for her, despite knowing better.

"The control of pain presented some difficulties, too. The medicines we used tended to make Mother groggy, so she tried to use as little as possible, torn between full but painful consciousness and partial loss of selfhood. The medicines were given by shots, and this in itself became increasingly painful to her. It was a problem we never fully resolved. [Since 1971, great improvements have been made in pain control. See page 15.]

"Through it all, Mother had a remarkably buoyant and outgoing spirit. Dad and I both felt that our investment of time and energy in home care was richly rewarded in family closeness, strength gained, and love expressed."

Stages of Dying

The Five Stages of Dying listed below were postulated by Elisabeth Kubler-Ross in her landmark book *On Death and Dying*. They are not to be taken as gospel, however, as she herself points out. They describe emotional responses commonly experienced by dying persons, but may be experienced very differently depending upon a person's particular illness, age, sex, personality, religious orientation, and situation.

In relating to a dying person it is helpful to realize that these reactions are normal and should be accepted. Not all of them will necessarily appear, nor will they necessarily appear in the order listed. No one should be expected or pushed to experience any of them, nor judged lacking for not experiencing one or more, including acceptance. Each person experiences death in a unique way.

A person who, through reading, discussion and reflection has accepted the reality and universality of death may soften or eliminate the negative reactions. That is one of the values of death education. Similarly, negative feelings often reflect the inability of those around a patient—family, friends and caretakers—to accept death. If others can accept the impending death and continue to relate warmly to the patient as a human being, he or she will also be able to accept the situation more easily.

These are the stages as set forth by Kubler-Ross:

Denial and isolation are often the first response to a terminal diagnosis. The patient will doubt the diagnosis or be convinced of the certainty of recovery. This can help to gain time for the person to assimilate the magnitude of the impending changes ("terror management"). This is different from the element of hope for recovery or reprieve which remains and is helpful even when death has been accepted.

Anger usually accompanies acceptance of the diagnosis and may be directed at medical personnel, family, friends, oneself, and God. Outwardly or inwardly the person feels resentment, perhaps rage, against the presumed causes of the disease, near or remote, against present care which is powerless to remove the apparent death sentence, and so on.

Bargaining is observed in the effort to make a deal with God, or with medical staff, or with the disease—to obtain more time.

Depression often replaces anger and bargaining as the probability of death is accepted. This may include feelings of remorse, unworthiness, and fear of death. Being able to experience and express this depression will help in moving beyond it, though it is likely to recur intermittently.

Acceptance may finally be reached, not as despair, but as detachment from people and things formerly valued, a quiet expectation of the step to come, however it may be conceived.

Dying persons should be allowed to accept the reality of their situation at their own pace. Information should neither be withheld from them nor thrust upon them. Ordinarily they will ask for it. Other people can help by making clear they are open to talk, by inviting conversation and responding honestly. Sharing of thoughts, questions, and feelings is a most important means for a person nearing death to make peace with the situation.

Unfinished Business

Dr. Kubler-Ross has pointed out the importance of encouraging and assisting dying people of any age to complete needed tasks and resolve relationships, including saying good-bye and making final arrangements and disposition of possessions. Identifying and completing this "unfinished business" helps bring an inner peace and acceptance of death. Frequently a person facing death reflects on his or her life, seeking a sense of meaning and perspective. Dr. Robert Butler points out that what may seem to be garrulousness may be part of this "life review." Others can help by allowing time for listening, reflection, and sharing, perhaps taking down memoirs by hand or tape.[1]

Honesty among family and friends about the dying person's situation is needed to make possible this completing of tasks, and to avoid later regret about lost opportunities for communication.

Deciding about Home Care

Home care is not for everyone. Some families may not have the physical and emotional resources. More than half of people in nursing homes have mental deterioration making them especially difficult to care for at home,[2] and half have no significant family relationship.[3] A family with children at home may find the demands too great if one of the parents requires intensive care.

People have varying capacities to accept the demands home care makes of caregivers. It is important to recognize and acknowledge when limits have been reached, when the cost to other family members has become too great, and when resentment may erode the quality of care. Especially when a patient no longer recognizes the caregiver, the services received may be more important than who gives them. In addition, some patients prefer the security of institutional care in serious illness. Social workers in hospitals, health departments and social service departments can suggest possible institutions. Resources to help in deciding are listed in Appendix 1, "Bibliography."

Help for Home Care

If you decide on home care, a variety of resources are available. Local health departments and home health agencies are good places to start. If there is a local home-care hospice and the patient is eligible for its services, that will assist greatly. Explore the resources of family, friends and religious organizations of which you are a member. Josefina Magno, first Executive Director of the National Hospice Organization, tells of a woman whose wish to die at home was realized because her synagogue organized help to assist with her care. There was no organized hospice at the time.

National sources for further information on home care are listed in Appendix 2, "Organizations." Associations for specific diseases can offer much pertinent advice. See Appendix 2, "Organizations." Be persistent in seeking what you need. Ask each source if they can suggest any other resource. Two very helpful books are *The 36-Hour Day: A Family Guide to Caring for Persons with Alzheimer's Disease, Related Dementing Illnesses, and Memory Loss in Later Life*, and *A Guide to Dying at Home*, both listed in Appendix 1, "Bibliography."

The Hospice Movement

In the Middle Ages hospice was the name given to a place of refuge—an inn—where travelers could refresh themselves on their journeys. The name was given a new meaning when St. Christopher's Hospice was formed in London in 1967 by Cicely Saunders. Hospice then became a place where the dying could live their remaining days as fully and comfortably as possible, surrounded by loved ones, free from pain, and dying with dignity. A few such freestanding hospices have been organized in the United States, and some hospitals have set aside wards for hospice care.

Most U.S. hospices, however, are organizations which help to care for patients in their own homes. Their goal is to provide care for the whole person—medical, physical, emotional, spiritual—relating to the whole family as the unit of care, through both the dying and a period of bereavement.

Beginning as predominantly volunteer programs, most hospice organizations now have a professional team, including a doctor who provides medical supervision, a nurse who monitors day-to-day care and coordinates the team, counselors (usually a social worker and/or pastor), and volunteers to assist and relieve the family as needed. The team works together to serve the family, learning from each other and seeking to provide a unified approach to care and treatment. Most hospices provide twenty-four hour, seven-day-a-week accessibility of services, since crises may arise at any time. There are now nearly 1700 such hospice organizations in the United States.

Eligibility

For a patient to be eligible for the services of most hospices, death must be anticipated within a limited time, usually six to twelve months. Eighty percent of hospice patients at this time are cancer patients, though persons with Alzheimer's, AIDS and other terminal conditions are also served.

Finding a Hospice Organization

To find out if there is a hospice organization in your area contact your local health department or the National Hospice Organization, or the state organization. See Appendix 3, "Hospice Organizations," To see if an organization will be able to meet your needs, you may want to know the composition of the hospice team, and the availability and training of volunteers.

Pain Control

Better ways of controlling pain in terminal illness have been a major contribution of the hospice movement. Using the same practices for chronic pain as are usual for acute care, as still often happens in hospitals, has led to a great deal of pain which could have been avoided. In hospice, chronic pain is controlled by giving sedatives on a regular basis, rather than waiting until the patient feels pain and asks for relief. This largely removes the fear and stress associated with chronic pain and may actually lessen the pain itself. Oral medicines are used rather than injections, which tend to become increasingly difficult. The key is careful combination of drugs and continuing precise adjustment of dosages as the condition of the patient changes.

Nutrition

Nutrition is another sensitive issue in terminal care. When the goal of patient care is recovery or prolongation of life, it is important for a patient to receive adequate nourishment. This in itself is difficult because seriously ill patients experience some loss of appetite. The patient will become less and less tolerant of food as his or her body deteriorates. When food is refused, caregivers often feel rejected or inadequate, being no longer able to offer this tangible comfort and fearing further decline of their loved one.

Hospice workers can offer help in maintaining good nutrition, and support and reassurance when this is no longer possible. In hospice care, as in hospital care, the question of artificial and/or forced feeding may arise. This raises complex questions for the patient, the family, and the hospice team, and no easy answers are available. Primary considerations should be respect for the wishes of the patient, and whether the benefits to be gained realistically outweigh the discomforts and cost. For further discussion, see Chapter 4, "The Right to Die."

Costs of Hospice Care

Not only are dying people commonly much happier at home but there can also be financial savings. Our little hospice organization here in Yancey County estimated that in the first 18 months of their operation they saved their patients $500,000 in hospital bills. Institutional hospice care, on the other hand, may cost as much or more than regular hospital care. For information on coverage of hospice care costs by Medicare, Medicaid and private insurance companies, see Appendix 3, "Hospice Organizations."

A Caution

We rejoice at the growth of the hospice movement and the opportunity it brings to many for a humane and dignified death. As with any service, however, the increasing quality of care that accompanies professionalization is not without costs, both human and financial. We must take care to retain sensitivity and flexibility in home care, and to avoid unthinking acceptance of high costs, just because we have grown accustomed to this in the acute care cost structure of hospitals. Ideally, the hospice movement will help all our health care institutions to become more responsive and flexible in meeting the needs of patients and their loved ones, not overwhelming the natural processes of life with complex technology.

Alzheimer's Disease

It is estimated that there are about four million persons with Alzheimer's disease in the United States in 1990, with no effective treatment or definitive diagnostic test available except at autopsy. It is the fourth leading cause of death among adults, with an as yet unknown origin. It produces progressive degeneration in the brain, called dementia, leading gradually to profound memory loss and eventually to complete helplessness. Some seventy percent of Alzheimer's patients are cared for at home, and are eligible for hospice care only in the final stages of the illness. The degenerative process lasts three to twenty years—eight to ten on the average—and caregivers usually experience many, often severe, stresses. Alzheimer's support groups are increasingly being formed, and excellent materials are available from the Alzheimer's Disease and Related Disorders Association, Inc. See Appendix 2, "Organizations."

Acquired Immunodeficiency Syndrome—AIDS

AIDS is a virus-caused disease first reported in 1981. According to the National AIDS Information Clearing House (see Appendix 2, "Organizations") there have been 133,889 known cases since the disease was discovered—though estimates run as high as a million. To date, 81,906, or 61.2 percent have died.

The virus breaks down the immune system, causing patients to be very susceptible to infections, especially the otherwise rare Kaposi sarcoma (a cancer) and pneumocystis carnii pneumonia. Some persons infected with the AIDS virus develop the less severe symptoms of the AIDS-related complex (ARC)—tiredness, fever, loss of appetite, diarrhea, night sweats, and swollen lymph glands.[4]

Most adult patients with AIDS live at home, with occasional hospitalization for acute episodes of illness. Some special considerations apply to home care of AIDS patients. The chance of a caretaker contracting AIDS is extremely low, since AIDS is spread primarily through sexual contact, use of contaminated IV needles, and blood transfusions. Because much is still unknown about transmission of AIDS, however, caution is advised. The Public Health Service now recommends that caretakers wear gloves to avoid contact of skin and mucous membranes with blood and body fluids of AIDS patients, and surfaces soiled with blood should be cleaned with a household disinfectant.

Caution is recommended also to help a person with AIDS avoid exposure to infections. A most helpful book is *Living with AIDS — A Self-Care Manual*, edited by Lang, Spiegel and Strigle, listed in Appendix 1, "Bibliography."

Obtaining appropriate health care and assistance from public and private agencies is often difficult. The "epidemic of anxiety" concerning AIDS causes capricious and demoralizing discrimination. Hospitals, dentists, ambulance services, welfare agencies, hospices, laundries and others may offer limited service or even refuse to serve a person with AIDS. However, the discrimination against AIDS patients is diminishing. Support groups and special advocates can help develop resources. There is no substitute for persistence in pursuing those services which are, or should be, available.

The National Hospice Organization adopted a policy in 1985 calling on hospices to serve AIDS patients, and most programs are now open to people with AIDS.

Completing of "unfinished business" may be a special challenge and opportunity for those with AIDS. For the sixty to sixty-five percent who are men and contracted the disease through sexual contact with another man, openness with family, friends and associates can present major difficulties. Near hysterical fear of the disease itself is frequently compounded by a phobic reaction to homosexuality. Reactions of family members may range from acceptance to shock and outrage, complicated by embarrassment about irrational responses. While not all alienation can be resolved, many have found that facing death brings forth unexpected love and reconciliation, even when disagreements remain. Helpful books and organizations are listed in Appendices 1 and 2, "Bibliography" and "Organizations."

The Dying Child

"All children know," Dr. Kubler-Ross says, "(not consciously, but intuitively) about the outcome of their illness. All little ones are aware (not on an intellectual, but on a spiritual level) if they are close to death." They are also aware of the pain and worries of their families and cannot be fooled about them. She counsels parents: "Tell them you are sad and sometimes feel so useless that you cannot help more. They will hold you in their little arms and feel good that they can help you by sharing comfort. Shared sorrow is much easier to bear than leaving them with feelings of guilt and fear that they are the cause of all your anxiety."[5]

While false cheer should be avoided, the family, and especially healthy children, should feel free to continue to laugh and play, bring friends home and lead a normal life as far as possible. "The worst thing we can do to the terminally ill child and the rest of the family is to make a morgue out of the house while the child is still living. Where there is laughter and joy, shared love, and little pleasures, the day-to-day difficulties are much easier to bear." Overprotection and overindulgence are to be avoided as confusing both to the sick child and to other children who are not similarly treated.

Brothers and sisters should be informed and "become part of the care in one way or another." At home, they can do tasks appropriate to their ages and even in the hospital they can make cheerful decorations or play favorite music on a tape recorder. "Such illnesses are much harder on the brothers and sisters than they are on the patient," Dr. Kubler-Ross comments. These siblings should have the support of a group or an adult to help them cope. They need special attention to their own situations and how they feel about what they are going through.

By continuing a normal family life as far as possible, and being sure that family members or friends spend extra time with healthy brothers and sisters, these children can share in the experience of caring, love and grief without feeling neglected or wishing the child would die so that normal family life could be resumed.

Support for families with children who are dying is as essential as in home care of an elderly person. Informal support structures or hospice organizations can offer strategic relief to the caregiving parent(s), and this is often overlooked.

General Comments on Dying

Kubler-Ross says "Those who have the strength and the love to sit with a dying patient in the silence that goes beyond words will know that this moment is neither frightening nor painful. ... Watching a peaceful death is like watching a falling star."[6]

"While death is easy, dying can be hard work," Deborah Duda adds.[7] Breathing may be labored or rasping, or quiet and spaced with long pauses. The person may grow colder and require additional covers, or may run a high fever and wish to shed coverings. Ice chips are good to relieve dryness of the mouth. There may be unusual or unpleasant odors. The patient may become somewhat disoriented or see hallucinations or visions. Most patients are comforted by the presence of a loved one, and many appreciate their hand being held. Persons who appear to be unconscious are sometimes aware of what is happening around them and what is being said. An elderly woman, apparently comatose, heard a nurse remark, "It's about time the old bitch died!" She later revived and mentioned the remark. It may be helpful to assure the dying person that those left behind will be all right, and that it is OK for him or her to let go and leave the body.

At death, as at birth, it is good to have someone present who has attended other deaths and knows what to expect. Hospice can be very helpful in this regard. Duda's book, quoted above, is specific and helpful. See Appendix 1, "Bibliography." Caretakers and family members need to provide for their own needs, especially if the dying is prolonged.

An important advantage of death at home is that family and friends may sit with the body for awhile. They may sit in silence, or talk to or about the patient, or pray. This time after death can be very helpful to survivors in beginning to adjust to the loss. This is an old practice in some cultures, and some hospitals and nursing homes will cooperate, especially if it is prearranged.

It is my feeling that family members, especially children, who are at hand when someone dies should be encouraged to see the person who has died, but should not be urged. This may help them accept the reality of the death. After a peaceful death, cosmetic restoration, which makes the person appear lifelike, detracts from the experience.

When my wife died, my daughter's two children were with me. I asked if they would care to see her before we put her body in the box. The girl said yes, the boy said no. That was all right on both counts. There was no cosmetic work and no public viewing. The whole thing was low-keyed and natural.

What is done next will depend on plans for the disposition of the body and for memorial or funeral services. See Chapter 5, "Simple Burial and Cremation;" and Chapter 7, "Death Ceremonies."

REFERENCES

[1]"Successful Aging and the Role of the Life Review," *Journal of the American Geriatrics Society*, 22:530, 1974.

[2]*Washington Post Health*, December 30, 1986, p.13

[3]Robert N. Butler, M.D., "The Need for Quality Hospice Care," address to National Hospice Organization, 1978, p.8.

[4]"Gay and Bisexual Men and AIDS", U.S. Public Health Service pamphlet, in *Latest Facts About Aids* series, October 1986.

[5]Quotations in this section are taken with permission from Elisabeth Kubler-Ross, *On Children and Death*. New York: Macmillan Publishing Co., 1983, pp.1-3.

[6]Elisabeth Kubler-Ross, *On Death and Dying*. New York: Macmillan Publishing Co., 1969, p.246.

[7]Deborah Duda, *Coming Home*. Santa Fe, New Mexico: Aurora Press, 1982, p.219.

3   BEREAVEMENT[1]

"It is this sorrow of separation ... this overspreading pain that deepens into loves and desires, into sufferings and joys in human homes; and this it is that ever melts and flows in songs through my poet's heart."　　　　　　　　　—*Rabindranath Tagore*

With every change we experience both gains and losses, and with the losses, grief, which is the process by which loss is healed. Some losses are small, passing almost unnoticed. Some are more serious —such as a divorce or the loss of a job or of a dream—and cause significant grief reactions. Some losses, such as the death of a loved one, are grievous. They cut us off from someone or something which gives life meaning, purpose or security. With such a loss, we lose a crucial part of ourselves. It is as if we experienced the death of those aspects of ourselves.

Grieving is the natural process by which a loss is healed. Understanding that there is a natural process to grieving can help us feel more in control and to have more trust as we move through it. As we allow ourselves to experience grief, and if we can find the needed support, we will find ourselves with greater compassion, deepened and enriched relationships with others, and a more vivid sense of the meaning and value of life.

Cultural Barriers to Grieving

Grieving can be difficult in our culture, where grief and pain are often taboo. Necessary emotional support may be lacking if family and friends, uncomfortable with the pain, avoid the grieving person or the topic of the loss. Well-meaning people may encourage us to deny how deep the pain really is. Religious beliefs may be construed to suggest that the pain is unreal or should be quickly healed. Secular therapies also may gently pressure us to "integrate" the experience.

As we avoid facile comfort, we can also avoid unnecessary anxiety by understanding the grief process. We can know that we are not "going crazy", and that the devastating pain will not last forever, despite our feelings to the contrary. We will know how to help ourselves, or others who grieve, and when special help is needed.

The Process of Grieving

Each person experiences loss in a unique way. At some time, however, most people will experience all of the following, some of them many times, and even after years have passed:

1. Denial, shock, numbness—protecting us from realization of the magnitude of the loss, especially in the case of sudden loss.
2. Emotional release—often a flood of tears, realization of loss, beginning of healing.
3. Depression, loneliness, isolation.
4. Physical symptoms—physical sensations: emptiness or hole in the pit of the stomach; lump in the throat; tightness in chest, sighing, tiring or weakness of body; lack of energy; dry mouth; headaches; etc. A wide variety of minor or serious digestive, respiratory, hormonal, cardiovascular, and immune system deficiency symptoms are possible.
5. Panic—when a person feels unable to cope with an unknown future, or that there is something wrong with her or him.
6. Remorse—ranging from the almost universal sense of one's shortcomings to the intense guilt often experienced on the loss of a child, or when there are unresolved conflicts, or in the case of suicide.
7. Anger—at the deceased for dying, or at anyone who might be blamed for the death, or at God. Also anger at self, and guilt—for all the things I should have done or said, or all the things I wish I hadn't done or said. This is normal, but may be difficult to face and share.
8. Need to talk—to express feelings, share memories, find meaning in the person's life.
9. Taking positive actions in response to a death—like working to avoid similar deaths for others, reaching out to persons similarly bereaved, completing projects of, or on behalf of, the deceased. This is always healing, but especially helpful for relief of guilt.
10. Readjustment—reaching out in new relationships and experiences.

My Own Experience

Again, I refer to my own family for experience in depth. When I was just a few months old my mother died, and my father and I went to live with his parents and his older sister, who became my foster mother.

My father remarked once, late in life, "When someone you love dies, your love doesn't die, it gets redistributed." Profoundly bereft by the loss of my mother, he became a gentler, more caring person.

Much of his affection and of his hopes and dreams centered on me. I can't recall being punished, or even scolded. Surrounded by loving adults I enjoyed an almost idyllic childhood. Discipline was no problem. I adored my father and was eager to do what he wanted. In a manner of speaking, my mother's death illuminated our lives.

Not until recent years did I realize that a warm and happy childhood had enhanced the sense of well-being which I enjoyed throughout a long life. The death of a loved one — or just the awareness of the inevitability of death — can deepen our relationships and enrich our appreciation of the daily experience of living.

The experience of death took a very different turn when, in my teens, I lost, through cancer, the beloved aunt who had cared for me from infancy. Sadly bereft, I meditated deeply on life and decided that the best thing I could do for her was to carry on her life. Not necessarily her specific ideas, but the quality of her life, which was characterized by integrity and a profound human dedication. After that my grief went away.

During and after my wife's death the bereavement was more profound. Together, over a period of forty years, we had homesteaded, raised a family, built a business, founded a school, and more. Together we had biked, canoed, camped and climbed mountains. Without her my life was suddenly empty. I worked through this grief in several ways over a period of years.

For me perhaps the most important form of release was in personal involvement. I helped take care of her before she died, helped lift her body into the box, and loaded it into my old station wagon. I drove to the burying ground, helped lower the box and recited her favorite poem about death.

A day or so later, we held a memorial meeting at the school, where I spoke for an hour and twenty minutes, telling of my wife's life. This did me a world of good. A few days later we held a meeting at Yellow Springs, Ohio, where we had lived most of our lives. Again, I spoke, but this time for only forty minutes! Men, in our culture, have been denied ready access to tears, and speaking may provide emotional release instead. The importance of this often is overlooked because women usually outlive their husbands and we tend to assume survivors are women.

While I was able to respond to the immediate challenge of my wife's death, I knew that unless special measures were taken I would become ill once life returned to normal. So, as quickly as possible, I set forth on a business trip, which would involve me in a tight schedule, associating closely with people. My health soon stabilized. I well remember my return from that trip. It was dusk, and as I drove down the mountain road toward home I thought sadly, "Elizabeth won't be there." The house was dark and I felt lonely. I phoned the school, which was nearby. "How about holding All-School Meeting at my house tonight?" I asked. Sure enough, a few minutes later students and staff arrived, filling the big music room, and a warm sense of fellowship came over me.

One aspect of bereavement that I had not anticipated was the loss of identity. With Elizabeth gone I was no longer me! After forty years of sharing on such a broad spectrum of life, I did not have a separate identity. This was not painful, nor did it interfere with my activities, but it was very strange, and several years were required to get over it. I understand this is more often experienced by men, while women may feel a stronger sense of being deserted.

Happy involvement with many friends and ongoing projects soon restored to me a sense of well-being. It seemed that I had handled my bereavement well, and I had, but my wife kept appearing in my dreams. She wasn't dead after all—she had merely been away. It seemed so real that the happiness of her return would linger after I awoke. Clearly I still had a long way to go.

Some seven years after her death I found myself attracted to a young woman who embodied some of Elizabeth's qualities. I had no idea of marrying her because of the age difference, but the attraction continued. I finally realized that I was, in effect, projecting my wife onto her—trying in this way to bring back Elizabeth. With time and effort I was able to realize this and let go of my wife. My attraction to the young woman then subsided to a cordial friendship. I was helped in this by being able to talk freely about it with my daughter.

Many years after Elizabeth's death, at age 77, I did marry again, very happily, a woman of my own age whom I had known in college, and who like myself had been widowed. We shared the same values and concerns. The marriage is a new one, not the reincarnation of an old one. In contemplating this marriage the problem of death gave me serious pause. Did I really want to become vulnerable to death once more? During my marriage with Elizabeth there was always the shadow of a fear that I might die first, thus deserting her. With her death, this shadow vanished and I no longer feared death. Did I really want to give hostage to life again? Finally I and my new love made peace with death and agreed to a marriage which would be temporary—until one of us died. We have deliberately accepted grief as part of life, and are happy.

Group Support in Bereavement

Group support is important for a family experiencing bereavement. (See Appendix 1, "Bibliography" and also Appendix 2, "Organizations."

It was a beautiful Sunday morning in 1966. I was in Ohio, on the phone with my wife in North Carolina. Suddenly an operator broke in with an emergency call from Detroit. Our younger daughter, age twenty-nine, had been killed in a motor accident.

First I called back to my wife and broke the news to her. That was the hardest part. We set up plans for her to fly to Ohio. Then I phoned one of our friends, who was a member of the Friends Meeting (Quaker), asking him to get the word to the other Meeting members. At 11:00 a.m. I went to Meeting. Not much was said, but I could feel the love and support. I still remember the words of a thoughtful young man who spoke. "Until we have learned to accept death we are not really living." I found this a comforting thought.

Later I met my wife at the airport and brought her home. As if by magic meals appeared, chores were done and errands run. Old friends came to see us. Hospitality was arranged for relatives from out of town. A memorial meeting was quietly arranged. We seemed to be carried along on a gentle wave of love. We never learned who coordinated that — probably several people helped.* The memorial meeting was a heartwarming affair, at which several people spoke, all spontaneously.

Looking back on that period, I am struck by the contrast with the occasion fifteen years earlier when we experienced another death in the family. At that time the members of the Meeting had been sympathetic, but there was no concerted move to give us the needed help. What had happened to change the situation so much for the better?

For one thing, the Meeting had established a committee to organize help for families at a time of death. From this had grown the habit of doing that, to the point where it happened almost spontaneously. The fact that I turned to the Meeting for help was probably important also. The habit of organizing immediate help for a family at a time of death is practiced in many religious groups. It is a good one to cultivate.

Another thing I would like to stress is the importance of visits by friends following a death. I recall an incident when my wife and I planned to visit a good friend whose husband had died, but were a bit slow in getting to it. When we finally did, she met us at the door, exclaiming, "I *knew* you'd come!" The bereaved person normally has feelings of insecurity and often of guilt as well. The attention of friends is very important. Simple communication of the feeling of caring is probably the most important thing that can be done in the first hours or days after a loss. When the survivor feels like talking or expressing feelings, the listening and acceptance of a friend will help understanding and healing to emerge from within.

---

*Arrangements for immediate cremation were made through a quick call to the Detroit Memorial Society. Memorial societies throughout the U.S. and Canada reciprocate in assisting one another's members. See Chapter 7, "Memorial Societies."

Children and Grief

Children, too, experience grief in a form depending on their age and circumstances. They, too, need to accept the reality of loss and to mourn in their own way. Efforts to protect children from grief by explaining death as sleep or a journey can result in serious confusion. A child's questions should be answered honestly, in language he or she can understand. By the age of five children can begin to understand the permanence of death. It may be helpful to tell the child that the body of a dead person is peaceful and feels no pain, and that the child did not cause the death. The adult's feelings about the loss, and her or his religious beliefs can also be shared in language understandable to the child. It is important to assure the child that she or he will be cared for and they and those they love kept safe. As important as the words is the feeling behind them. The adult's acceptance of death, and faith in the future, will be conveyed to the child.

The natural anger often expressed by children at the loss of a sibling, parent, grandparent or friend may be shocking to adults. Earl Grollman's *Talking About Death* gives useful guidelines for helping children deal with their anger, sadness and guilt. See Appendix 1, "Bibliography." The pain and anger of a bereaved child may be expressed in nightmares, inability to concentrate, moodiness, uncharacteristic roughness or violence. Children need an opportunity to acknowledge and express the complex feelings of bereavement. They can be helped, too, to understand the grief reactions of those around them. It is important that they be encouraged to feel free to continue enjoying their lives despite the loss which has occurred. Sometimes it helps for a family member or friend to explain to school personnel what is happening. See Appendix 1, "Bibliography," for other books to help children with loss.

The Death of a Child

The grief experienced by parents when a child dies is particularly severe. Even if the child was an adult, loss of the hopes and dreams embodied in the child, and sudden inability to continue the caring and nurture in which a parent's life is invested combine to prolong and intensify grief. The assistance of a support group or professional counselor often helps to meet these challenges, and to allow the parents to emerge from the tragedy strengthened and with a stronger relationship. It may be wise to begin such help as soon as the death is anticipated, even when there appears to be no problem. To locate parent groups, see listings in Appendix 2, "Organizations."

When a child is lost, the relationship of parents is placed under special stress, too, because the normal support, reassurance, and intimacy of the relationship may also seem to be lost or threatened. The anger that is a normal part of grieving may be directed against a spouse. Each may experience the pain of seeing the other suffer, and feel unable to help. And each will grieve in a different way, at a different pace. This can easily create tension and misunderstanding. The spouse, or other children, may remind a parent of the lost child, creating more pain within the family where one formerly turned for comfort.

It will help to realize that the couple relationship needs to be given priority, and to take time to listen, to share, to have fun together, to continue to touch and hug each other, and to renew other aspects of the relationship. Each needs to cultivate patience, to allow space in the relationship, and to realize that the spouse cannot be the only source of healing.

Once again, with understanding and time the loss can help illuminate their lives, helping them to become more loving and patient. I know a father who loved his children, but was somewhat rough with them. Losing one through drowning, he suddenly realized what they meant to him and became kind and gentle. As a boy I lost a baby sister through the Sudden Infant Death Syndrome. It was totally unexpected, and a great shock to us. Before the baby was taken away, my parents and I stood with our arms around each other—looking at the baby. That was a precious moment, filled with grief and love. The death of a child can draw a family together in warmth and tenderness.

The death of an infant before or shortly after birth is also an occasion for profound grief, complicated by the fact that society either may not recognize the loss or may regard it as a misfortune from which parents will quickly recover. Such a loss may happen suddenly and be a young family's first experience with death. They are likely to be unprepared for the strength and persistence of their grief. Family and friends may find it especially hard to recognize and accept the grief of fathers whose babies die.

Both parents should be encouraged to see the child, to name him or her, and accept the reality of the child as a member of the family. It may help to have the hospital take the usual newborn photograph, and to save this along with the baby's hospital bracelet. Holding and being alone with the baby for a time may help. Not to recognize the existence and the loss of a child in such ways often results in parents' inability to accept the reality of the loss. This is reinforced by our general practice of acting as if an infant who dies has never existed.

The National Funeral Directors Association suggests that parents can be helped by "considering holding/dressing/casketing of the infant," as well as by "developing meaningful rites and rituals that involve the parents, grandparents and siblings as participants and not mere observers."[2] Friends can help by acknowledging the event by words or caring gestures.

Loss of a child through abortion or adoption needs also to be mourned. Not only mothers, but fathers also frequently experience deep feelings of loss. Again, each must grieve the loss in his or her own way and time.

Suicide Survivors

Those bereaved by a suicide are often called "survivor victims" because of the intensified guilt, anger and social stigma they experience. Healing includes the realization that the roots of suicide are complex and no one, including parents and spouse, should be blamed. For a discussion of suicide prevention, see Chapter 5, "The Right to Die." See also Appendix 2, "Organizations," for a list of support groups.

AIDS Survivors

When someone with AIDS (acquired immunodeficiency syndrome) has died, bereavement is likely to have additional complications. Typically, those who die from AIDS are young, some in the midst of promising careers, with a whole future to be mourned. The intense fears and stigma often attached to the disease can make it extremely difficult for survivors to be open about their loss, greatly intensifying the loneliness and isolation typically felt by the bereaved. The support normally extended to the bereaved can be overwhelmed by negative attitudes, and practical arrangements are often greatly complicated. (See Chapter 5, "Simple Burial and Cremation," for help with funeral arrangements for AIDS victims.) Many resources which have been developed for AIDS patients and survivors are an outgrowth of the gay community and are less likely to serve others who are affected.

Special Issues for Bisexual or Homosexual Men

The family and friends of homosexual or bisexual AIDS patients may have to deal for the first time or in a new way with feelings concerning the person's lifestyle. Guilt and regrets for past decisions and attitudes may be intensified. Sadly, a surviving friend or lover may be excluded from funeral arrangements as family members assume the legal responsibility for disposition of the body, perhaps in violation of the expressed wishes of the one who has died. The loss may cause the survivor to lose his straight identity and to have to deal with resulting prejudice and discrimination. A surviving lover will face his own fears of contagion, and the normal resumption of social life will carry the added heavy burden of being a possible carrier of AIDS. Multiple losses may occur within one's social group, creating the feeling that one's whole community is a "sinking ship". Support groups exist in some urban areas, but many areas lack appropriate resources. Helpful written materials are available from the National AIDS Information Clearing House. See Appendix 2, "Organizations." See also Appendix 1, "Bibliography."

Other Situations of Bereavement

The impact of death touches others besides family and friends. In accidents or disasters, emergency workers need to give attention to their own emotional reactions, as well as to the needs of the survivors. Those who cause the death of another are likely to feel intense guilt, which is itself a genuine and often devastating form of grief.

When my younger daughter was killed by a drinking driver, he wrote us a letter telling us how terrible he felt. This was helpful to us, and, I imagine, also to him. Thinking about it afterwards, it might have been helpful to have responded, acknowledging his grief in the situation.

When the *legal responsibility* for an accident is not clear, regret can be expressed in a way which neither accepts nor denies such responsibility. In these situations, as with the loss of a loved one, it is important to take time to be aware of the feelings and to accept feelings such as shock and grief, even when they are unexpected. Again, the best comfort one can offer is usually simply to be present and accepting, listening rather than telling, as the person experiences the varied aspects of grief.

Support Groups and Professional Help

Bereaved people often find peer support groups of great help in dealing constructively with their loss. Such groups exist for widows, parents who have lost newborns, infants or older children, survivors of suicide and murder, and others. The National Self-Help Clearing House can help locate additional support groups, including groups for parents or patients with many diseases, injuries, or handicapping conditions. See Appendix 2, "Organizations." Books and pamphlets for the bereaved are available from these organizations and some are listed in the Bereavement section of Appendix 1, "Bibliography."

A professional experienced in bereavement counseling can also provide healing assistance through the grief process. Acting as a guide, a professional can help the bereaved with unfinished business and saying good-bye.

Professional evaluation is indicated if a person experiences incapacitating depression, panic, unusual guilt or excessive anger. Gradual or sudden onset of illness, or weight gain or loss in excess of fifteen pounds are other signs that help may be needed. Prolonged lack of any feeling or continued denial of the loss also suggests need for professional assistance.

Good Physical Care

Research has demonstrated that grieving persons who take good physical care of themselves are more likely to avoid serious problems. This includes maintaining a balanced diet; paying attention to thirst and drinking adequate fluids to avoid dehydration (caffeine and alcohol act as diuretics and tend to increase dehydration); engaging in regular exercise; and resting when tired, rather than pushing to keep going.

Avoid the Use of Drugs

Tranquilizers are sometimes prescribed for persons in grief. These may be helpful as a temporary measure, but they numb feelings and tend to prevent the "grief work" that must be done. If medication becomes more than temporary, professional counseling should be sought.

Catastrophic Loss

Individual responses to loss can be multiplied in social upheavals to become powerful social and political forces. As an administrator of refugee relief in the Middle East in 1950, I was responsible for 25,000 homeless people. I became acutely aware of the grief they felt. The loss of home, country, livelihood and sometimes of family members as well, represented great bereavement. Many clung to denial, fantasizing a return to the homeland. There was a vast reservoir of bitterness and anger against those who were blamed. I believe that terrorism, nationalism and warfare grow, in part, from these collective grief responses.

Along this line, many forces in our modern world create tragedy on a massive scale — shrinking forests; displaced cultures; expanding deserts; rising populations; millions of refugees from starvation, war and genocide; vast poverty and exploitation. Thus we find grief far beyond the normal — grief which must be dealt with at its roots. It is the responsibility of all of us to seek healing for this in whatever ways we can.

Bereavement Overload

It sometimes happens that deaths of friends and loved ones are so numerous or so frequent that the individual hasn't the time or resources needed for healing. In such cases, we should reach out to one another and make the best of the situation.

How Death Illuminates Life—An Example

"When someone you love dies, your love doesn't die, it gets redistributed." My father made this comment late in life on the occasion of a memorial service for a young woman. His own life was eloquent testimony to this.

My mother, reportedly a lovely and talented young woman, died of typhoid fever when I was a few months old. My father and I went to live with his parents and his older sister, who became my foster mother for the first six years of my life.

Sorely bereft, my father directed much of his affection toward me and I enjoyed an almost idyllic childhood. With advancing years, I realize more and more how much that childhood experience enriched my entire life. Nor was I the only beneficiary, as my father grew into a warmer and more caring person. He did not seek to avoid grief but was able to make grief a creative force in his life. In a profound way my mother's death illuminated our lives.

It can be helpful for survivors at a time of death to be aware of this potential and to draw strength and comfort from it. No one lives a full life without the experience of suffering. Whether we wither inside and are crippled by it, or reach out and grow with it, depends in large part on our understanding and our ability to let ourselves feel our pain and grow through our grief.

REFERENCES

[1]We are especially indebted for help with this chapter to Donna O'Toole of the Rainbow Connection, and Alexis Stein, of TO LIFE.

[2]National Funeral Directors Association, "Sudden Infant Death," 1981.

4   THE RIGHT TO DIE

This chapter discusses the right of patients to refuse treatment, and the importance and methods of advance planning. It discusses suicide and suggests how to communicate effectively with potential suicides. It discusses the issue of assisted suicide, offers ground rules for self-termination, and speaks out against life-denying habits which account for most self-destruction. It urges that compassion and common sense be used in making difficult decisions of principle.

The Right to Refuse Treatment

This matter has been given new urgency by the increasing availability of medical technology which, in the name of lifesaving, commonly prolongs the process of dying, often at great cost in suffering and expense. At issue is the right and ability of a dying person to remain in charge of his or her body, choosing when to fight for life and when to be allowed to die. Now that 80 percent of the two million annual deaths in the United States occur in institutions, a whole team of professionals must often be persuaded to refrain from doing what they are trained to do.

According to the American Medical Association at least ten thousand people are now being kept alive in permanently comatose condition with no prospect of recovery, and at a cost of hundreds of millions of dollars per year. Furthermore, as I commented in a previous chapter, some of these people, though totally unable to respond, may actually be aware of their circumstances and be leading a miserable existence.

The cost of futile death-prolonging treatment is often tremendous. An estimated 40 percent of the average American's lifetime expense for medical care is spent in his or her last thirty days.[1]

The right to refuse treatment is based on the common-law right of self-determination and the constitutionally derived right of privacy. As long as the patient understands the nature and consequences of refusing treatment and can communicate those wishes, the patient's wishes control, even if doctors or family disagree. Violation of a patient's expressed decision can subject health-care providers to civil damages. Patients who are competent do not lose this right upon becoming incompetent, provided they have indicated their wishes in writing and had them endorsed by their next of kin and family physician.

Families and physicians sometimes override a patient's wishes for a variety of reasons, although this violates the patient's legally protected rights. Families may be unable to accept the death of a loved one and to let the person go, or to risk the guilt of failing to do everything possible for the dying person, or simply to agree among themselves as to the best course of action. More commonly a dying person did not indicate his or her wishes in the past and is unable to do so in the present. Medical personnel fear legal liability should any family member later question a decision to withhold or withdraw care.

Hospital personnel and procedures are focused on keeping people alive. To permit a death which could have been postponed may seem a failure, a violation of regulations, or unethical. Measures begun under pressure of an emergency become difficult for family and physician to discontinue. Under these circumstances, a patient who wishes to refuse treatment is too often regarded as unruly and is restrained or drugged to make him or her more tractable.

Discuss It In Advance!

It is of utmost importance to discuss these matters in advance and to record decisions in writing. This allows family members to anticipate and adjust themselves to possibilities in advance, and to make peace, even if not in total agreement with the dying person's wishes. As I said before, it means a great deal to a dying person if his or her family is able to accept the death. Similarly, if a person wishes to cut short a painful and costly dying process, the situation is eased by family acceptance of this decision.

Finances are a legitimate concern. Some people will choose not to exhaust their savings in expensive and painful efforts to prolong life for a brief period, when they feel these resources could be better used for the lives of their loved ones.

Important also is frank and ongoing discussion with the doctor concerning the patient's condition and prospects, and feelings concerning terminal care. Such openness should begin early as it tends to become more difficult later on, especially for physicians under the intense pressures faced when providing critical care in a hospital. Most doctors appreciate the family taking the initiative in this as many find it difficult to do so and are unlikely to raise these questions.

If the ill or hospitalized person, or the family, feels at odds with the doctor after discussing the matter, it is proper to ask him or her to transfer the case to another doctor who will comply with the patient's wishes. If the doctor declines, ask the hospital administration to make the change. If they are unwilling, the matter may be taken to court to force the hospital either to honor the patient's wishes or to transfer him or her promptly to a complying physician.

"Living Will" and Power of Attorney

The way to formalize one's wishes is to write them in a Living Will declaration specifying limits to treatment in the event of serious and irreversible illness. These are recognized by statutes in most states, and forms complying with each of these various laws are available from The Society for the Right To Die. See Appendix 2, "Organizations".

Appendix 4, "Living Will," includes the standard Living Will Declaration, along with an Alternative Living Will which my wife and I have signed, and which goes somewhat further.

It is important that your Living Will be endorsed by your close relatives and by your doctor, and that it be witnessed by persons to whom you are not related by blood or marriage or who might in any way have an interest in your demise. Opposition to the Living Will is mainly based on the concern that relatives might seek to hasten a person's death for selfish reasons.

Artificial feeding remains a major issue. In some states it has been specifically exempted from Living Will directives in compliance with the wishes of some "right to life" groups. Recent court decisions, however, have upheld the right of patients to refuse artificial feeding. If your state declaration does not clearly express your wishes, you may do so in an added statement on the form.

You should be as specific as possible about the type of treatment you especially do not want (e.g., artificial feeding and fluids, antibiotics, chemotherapy, surgery, cardiac resuscitation). You should also be as specific as possible about the type of condition or quality of life in which you would not want to be artificially maintained (e.g., permanent unconsciousness, severe dementia, end-stage AIDS with periods of lucidity).

The U.S. Supreme Court decision in the *Cruzon* case forbade the removal of the stomach tubes which kept the incurably comatose woman alive on the grounds that, while she was quoted as having been opposed to such a procedure, she had left no written statement to that effect. She may have thirty years to go in this condition, and at a cost of some $100,000 a year.

At the same time, the court broke new ground in affirming the right of a patient to refuse treatment and to leave written instructions to that effect.

So, if you dislike the idea of your dying being dragged out for weeks, or months, or years, record your wishes *now*, in writing, and be sure they are available in case they are needed.

If you wish to donate organs and tissues, a statement to this effect needs to be added to your declaration, authorizing necessary maintenance of the body until needed organs and tissues can be removed. Suggested wording is provided in Appendix 4, "Living Will."

Living Will declarations can be backed up by a Durable Power of Attorney (DPA) authorizing a family member or friend to make health care decisions on your behalf should you be unable to do so. All states now make provision for such powers of attorney, and a few include this in their Living Will declarations. The making of health-care decisions, including the authority to forego life support, must be explicitly authorized. A suggested form is available from the Hemlock Society (address in Appendix 2, "Organizations"), but it is advisable to consult a local attorney because legal requirements vary greatly from state to state.

It is best to appoint the same proxy in all documents, and to specify a second proxy to act if the first one is not available when needed. The proxy may be a spouse, relative or friend, although a few states limit who may be appointed. Bear in mind that this person may have to make difficult and painful decisions on your behalf. It is vital to discuss your treatment preferences with the proxy to make sure he or she understands your wishes and is willing to advocate on your behalf in an undoubtedly stressful situation.

It is important that copies of these documents be given to close relatives or friends, to any proxy you have appointed, and to your doctor. Equally important, they should be included with your hospital chart if you are admitted to a hospital. If you change doctors, make sure your new doctor has a copy.

Support for the Right to Die

There is increasing support for the idea that the lives of terminally ill patients should not be prolonged by treatment against their will, or the will of their family or designee if the patient is unable to decide. For instance, the American Medical Association's Council on Ethical and Judicial Affairs issued a statement on March 15, 1986, declaring that artificially supplied respiration, nutrition and hydration may be withheld from a patient in an irreversible coma, even if death is not imminent. "In treating a terminally ill or irreversibly comatose patient," the Council said, "the physician should determine whether the benefits of treatment outweigh its burdens."

As courts increasingly uphold the right to refuse treatment, a number of cases around the country seek monetary damages from physicians and hospitals for not honoring a patient's rejection of treatment.

Although there are many variations of opinion, major Jewish and Protestant groups agree with the position of Pope Pius XII when he said in 1957 that in preserving life, "Normally one is held to use only ordinary means — according to circumstance, to persons, places, times, and culture — that is to say, means that do not involve any grave burden for oneself or another."

Sensitivity is Needed

While the principles may seem clear, many problems arise in carrying them out. It is not always clear when a condition is terminal or irreversible. Families and physicians need to be alert, too, to contradictory feelings in the patient who expresses a wish to be allowed to die. Temporary depression, unmet emotional needs, inadequate pain relief, and exaggerated fear of treatments sometimes enter in and should be considered before a decision is made.

The law is clear, however, that your wishes must be respected as long as you understand the nature of the treatment and the consequences of accepting or refusing it, and can communicate your decision. Other emotional, psychological, or intellectual problems are irrelevant as a matter of law.

It is important that sensitivity, compassion and goodwill are exercised, along with common sense, and that general rules are not rigidly applied.

The Dutch Example

Active euthanasia is practiced in Holland, where some ten thousand people a year obtain "death on request" — about one death in fifteen. The practice is still not legal, but no one is prosecuted for it if the rules have been followed.

The rules are very strict. Only the patient may ask for his or her death. No member of the family may ask for it and the physician may not suggest it. Indeed, the patient must ask for it several times and the physician must agree that the request is a reasonable one. He must know the patient well and must consult with another physician before carrying out the request. The physician and the family members are routinely interrogated by the police.

In some ways the circumstances are more favorable in Holland than in some other countries. Everyone is guaranteed public health insurance, so the dread of financial disaster does not hang over the family as sometimes happens in America. Then, too, the relationship between doctor and patient in Holland tends to be somewhat closer and more long-lasting than here. Dutch culture, by and large, tends to be marked by gentleness and integrity. Some eighty percent of Dutch people favor the privilege of "death on request."

Other countries, at first critical, are showing interest in the development and will no doubt follow suit in the course of time.

The Problem of Suicide[2]

The right to a merciful death for the terminally ill should not be confused with ending a life because of depression or failure to see other ways out of overwhelmingly painful circumstances. While the rate of suicide for all ages in the United States grew by 11% between 1950 and 1980, especially tragic was the 284% increase during the same period in suicides by people 15 to 24 years of age.[3]

Each year more than 5,000 people under the age of 24 kill themselves in the United States, and experts assume that a significant number of deaths recorded as accidents are actually suicides. When one adds unsuccessful suicide attempts, ten percent of students in high school and college may be at risk of suicide.[4] For ages 15 to 24 it is the third leading cause of death.

The transition from childhood to adulthood is an increasingly difficult period for many in our culture. Adolescents face many losses at a time when their accustomed sources of support may be weakest. Growing up means the loss of childhood — its innocence, freedoms, body image, relationships, and identity. The normal loosening of parental ties comes just as the young person is likely to meet intensified competition, hazing from peers, and loss of accustomed self-confidence. The relative security of the adult identity gained through such things as employment, marriage, children, and community involvements is not yet open to most teenagers in our high-tech, education-prolonging society.

With time and experience, most of us learn that even profound grief is not permanent, that eventually light will return to our lives. Adolescents often lack this perspective and are likely to have extreme reactions to loss, particularly because adolescence by its very nature is a time of extremes. Experiences such as a broken relationship, family quarrel, academic failure, or derision from peers may seem a final blow with no hope for a new beginning. For many, the possibility of nuclear catastrophe contributes to the difficulty in imagining a future for themselves. When life seems meaningless or overflowing with pain and stress, death may appear a logical choice. For the moment, the young person cannot see the irreplaceability of each human life, the fullness of life lived through and beyond pain, and the profound depth of suffering that such a death brings to others.

One vital challenge to modern education and family life, at least in the industrialized countries, is to involve young people in the work of the world in a meaningful way. Remembering how skillfully my parents did this for me I realize in hindsight what it meant to my emotional well-being and sense of belonging.

Another key challenge, especially to educational institutions, is to cultivate among students a spirit of mutual affirmation and support, rather than one of competition and "put-downs." Success in this area can contribute enormously to a feeling on the part of the young that life is really worthwhile. The Arthur Morgan School, which originally published this book through Celo Press, stresses the importance of meeting these two challenges.

Help will come, too, from learning to handle grief at all stages of life, accepting it as a natural and inevitable part of being alive. In this way we can learn to help ourselves and others express and release their feelings, and thus transform the pain of losses into growth, rather than depression or despair.

While we try to do all that may be possible to reduce stresses and provide supportive situations for young people generally, and those nearest us in particular, we can also seek to open our ears and our hearts to their thoughts and feelings. Especially we can be aware of danger signals, the "cry for help" that usually precedes suicidal actions. Take seriously expressions of despair, such as that life is hard and the future offers little hope, that one is weary of the struggle—no matter how unfounded others may feel these feelings to be. Inability to concentrate and recent excessive use of alcohol or drugs may be warning signs. Statements such as "death is peace, or reunion," or "suicide is a reasonable alternative" are strong signals. Do not hesitate to seek professional help if such feelings persist despite supportive efforts of family and friends.

All of this can be very difficult to do. Parents' relationship with adolescents are likely to be strained. Real openness to the struggles of teenagers raises painful or unresolved issues for most adults, among them the handling of sexual feelings and relationships, dreams and disappointments in work and careers, acceptance or rejection by peers, academic and social competition, experiences of loss, and so on. The willingness to struggle and grow in one's own life is necessary if one is to accept and share the feelings of another without minimizing them ("it's really not so bad"), or offering unhelpful advice or solutions ("just concentrate on your work and forget about him or her"). Studies suggest that when others accept the reality of a person's suicidal feelings, the chances of actual suicide are lessened.[5,6]

Focusing on the problem of suicide among young people should not cause us to lose sight of the need for much more attention to and understanding of self-destruction at any age. Suicide must be considered on a case by case basis if we are to truly learn its meaning and effectively develop ways to prevent it. Therefore, this discussion should be considered as only an introduction to a complex area of human life. Readers are urged to see the references in Appendix 1, "Bibliography," both "General" and "Right to Die."

Ground Rules for Self-Termination

While strongly disapproving of suicide in most cases, I would point out that a rule intended to prevent one form of tragedy, if arbitrarily applied, may lead to other and worse forms of tragedy.

I hold that, for the terminally ill, the deliberate ending of one's life is sometimes a good and wise act. Since the word suicide carries overtones of tragedy and disgrace, it may be helpful to use a less judgmental word to apply to wise self-termination. I am concerned here with the difficult task of formulating principles to govern the decision for or against self-termination by those with drastic disability or incurable illness.

1. A decision to end one's life should *never* be carried out at a time of depression or despair. Likewise, pathological motives, such as a desire to hurt someone, should be guarded against.
2. Pain control should be double-checked. People are sometimes driven to suicide by chronic pain that can be relieved by change of treatment.
3. One's social role and relationships should be taken into account. Being a living burden on a loving family may be better than leaving and may be less burdensome than the feelings experienced by the survivors following the commonly misunderstood act of "auto-euthanasia" (suicide). This is an individual and family matter. The conservation of social resources may be considered, too—energy, money and medical resources.
4. The decision to end one's life should rest with the person in question, and the means for doing so should be in his or her hands.

Some Examples

An elderly doctor, learning that he had an incurable cancer, determined to enjoy fellowship with his family to the fullest during his remaining months of life, and then, at the onset of his final decline, and with their consent, to quietly end his life with an appropriate drug. Thus he would spare himself and them the pain and expense of going the hard way. The family agreed and their last months together were deeply happy. His death did not involve suffering and his family, while they experienced grief and loneliness, did not suffer from shock or a sense of guilt.

Conversely, a doctor in my family, when asked by patients to help end their lives, would tell them which medicine, if taken all at once, would be lethal. The sense of empowerment that this gave to the patients, who no longer felt helpless, apparently helped restore the will to live. None of them took the medicine.

Similarly, I had a letter once from a woman I had never seen, who had a terminal illness and wished to cut it short. She said that none of her friends or family would talk with her about it, and asked if I would correspond with her—which I did. Exchanging letters, we discussed the pros and cons of ending her life and the various ramifications involved. I neither encouraged nor discouraged her. After awhile she decided on religious grounds that she would rather stick it out and let nature take its course.

A Personal Message

The following letter was written by an elderly physician.[7]

To the Editor:

As one who has had a long, full, rich life of practice, service, and fulfillment, whose days are limited by a rapidly growing, highly malignant sarcoma of the peritoneum, whose hours, days, and nights are racked by intractable pain, discomfort and insomnia, whose mind is often beclouded and disoriented by soporific drugs, and whose body is assaulted by needles and tubes that can have little effect on the prognosis, I urge medical, legal, religious and social support for a program of voluntary euthanasia with dignity. Prolonging the life of such a patient is cruelty. It indicates a lack of sensitivity to the needs of a dying patient and is an admission of refusal to focus on a subject that the healthy cannot face. Attention from the first breath of life through the last breath is the doctor's work; the last breath is no less important than the first.

Consent by the patient with a clear understanding of this act, by the patient's immediate family, by the family physician, lawyer, minister, or friend should violate no rules of social conduct. There is no reason for the erratic, painful course of the final events of life to be left to blind nature. Man chooses how to live; let him choose how to die. Let man choose when to depart, where, and under what circumstances. The harsh winds that blow over the terminus of life must be subdued.

Frederick Steen, M.D.
1240 West Park Avenue
Highland Park, IL 60036

Helping Someone to Die

A man I knew, in the final stages of cancer, asked his friends to bring him a drug with which he could end his life. This they did, but being very conscientious and wishing to be aboveboard, they notified the authorities about what they were doing. The sheriff's deputies rushed to the scene, but too late — the man was dead. No action was taken against the friends. Statistics gathered by the Hemlock Society indicate this type of action is increasing.

Many cases of mercy killings have been reported. Compassionate doctors and family members undoubtedly do it more often than we know. One young man even honored his hospitalized mother's request to shoot her. A number of people have been brought to trial for such actions, but they usually pled guilty and received noncustodial punishment, with the exception of two cases recently in which the accused received sentences of 15 years and 25 years.[8] Clearly, it is the more dramatic type of mercy killing, such as shooting, which tends to call forth legal action, rather than "gentler" procedures such as the administration of drugs.

A Legal Dilemma

Is it better to let "assisted suicide" remain outlawed, and then be humanely discriminating in enforcing the law, or to change the law itself? There is something to be said on both sides. Americans Against Human Suffering, for instance, proposes a national Humane and Dignified Death Act to legalize physicians' assistance to a patient in dying. The Hemlock Society (of which I am a member) provides counsel, information and literature. A good discussion of legal considerations, "Euthanasia, Aiding Suicide and Cessation of Treatment," 1982, is available free by mail from the Law Reform Commission of Canada, 130 Albert Street, Ottawa, Ontario K1A 0L6. See Appendix 1, "Bibliography," "Right to Die."

"Respectable" Forms of Suicide

No thoughtful discussion of suicide is complete that does not make reference to people who kill themselves a little every day. While society deplores "sudden suicide," it ordinarily condones the "slow suicide" implicit in a wide range of life-denying habits. Heart disease, for instance, our number one killer, can be greatly reduced by wholesome eating, appropriate exercise, avoiding overweight and steering clear of tobacco. The second killer, lung cancer, in eighty-eight percent of cases is attributed to smoking. The third killer, automobile injuries (about 50,000 deaths per year in the U.S.) can be cut more than half by the use of seat belts and by not drinking. Jellinek's disease (alcoholism) afflicts some 12 million people in the United States. It is said to shorten life by ten to twelve years and is involved in many auto accidents, eighty percent of home violence, thirty percent of suicides, sixty percent of child abuse, and sixty-five percent of drownings. Its economic cost is calculated at $54.1 billion annually. It is difficult to cope with because most sufferers firmly deny they have it.[9] The fourth killer, cirrhosis of the liver, is also associated with drinking.

The fifth killer, strokes, is commonly related to excess weight, as is hypertension, which is a frequent cause of strokes. Venereal disease is making a frightening comeback. The Centers for Disease Control reported a sharp increase in syphilis in the U.S. in 1980, and *The New York Times* reports gonorrhea as the most common bacterial disease of humans, with an estimated 50 million cases worldwide. Even more devastating is AIDS, which is assuming epidemic proportions and for which there is no known cure. All of these can be prevented.

The widespread excess consumption of sugar and caffeine also is conducive to degenerative disease. It is said that each of us consumes our weight in sugar annually. Heroin and other drugs claim thousands of lives and diminish the quality of life of thousands more. Increasingly, also, the pollution of our environment is taking a toll of life and health.

In short, self-destruction is rampant in our society. Why do people indulge in life-denying habits and needlessly dangerous acts? Is it in part because they do not accept the reality of death? They think they are defying death, whereas they are actually denying it. It is commonly the person who has been most careless in his or her habits who, when the chips are down, clings most desperately to the shreds of life. Those who have lived fully and are at peace with their lives can most easily face death, including the choice of a time for its ending.

REFERENCES

[1]*Yankee* magazine, "Man at the Crossroads," May 1984, p. 167.

[2]For help in understanding adolescent suicide we are indebted to Dr. John Schneider, *Finding My Way: Loss and Growth Across the Life Span*,unpublished manuscript, 1987.

[3]"Why 30,000 Americans will commit suicide this year," *U.S. News & World Report*, Vol.96, April 2, 1984, p.48.

[4]Michael Peck, "Youth Suicide," *Death Education*, 6:1, Spring 1982, p.29.

[5]Jonelle Timlin, "Study Shows Most Counselors Favour Change in Euthanasia Laws," *Hemlock Quarterly*, Jan.1983. Cites study showing that ignoring or rejecting someone's expressed desire to die is more likely to result in suicide.

[6]S.L. Dubovsky, "Averting Suicide in Terminally Ill Patients," *Psychosomatics*, Vol.9, No.2, 1978, pp.113-5, showed decreased likelihood of suicide in patients allowed to openly discuss suicide.

[7]Quoted with permission from *New England Journal of Medicine*, Letters to the Editor, 303:15, Nov.9, 1980, p. 891.

[8]Letter from Hemlock Society, March 3, 1987.

[9]*Newsweek*, October 17, 1983.

5   SIMPLE BURIAL AND CREMATION

This chapter discusses funeral costs and how to control them; how to get dignity, simplicity and economy in funeral arrangements; the options for body disposal; the values of simplicity; and the importance and methods of planning. It also discusses financial planning including prepayment plans, outlines things to be done at time of death, and tells about funerals conducted without funeral directors.

For help in preparing this chapter I am indebted to Harvey Lapin, general counsel to the Cremation Association of North America and the Prearrangement Interment Association of America; the National Funeral Directors Association; the Continental Association of Funeral and Memorial Societies; Howard Raether, former Executive Director of the National Funeral Directors Association, and Rev. Henry Wasielewski, of The Coalition for Fair Funeral Prices.

Despite soaring funeral costs nationally, it need not always be expensive to arrange for burial, cremation, or donation of a body.

In Celo Community, for instance, where I live, the complete cost of burial in the our community cemetery is about $25. This is made possible by a committee of our Quaker Meeting which provides moral and practical support to families at times of death. In addition to assisting with meals, child care, hospitality and other necessary paperwork, the committee quickly puts together a simple plywood box, digs a grave, and handles the burial. Family and close friends who wish to may view the body before burial, without cosmetic preparation. Later a memorial service is held focusing on the life and personality of the one who has died and on the spiritual aspect of the occasion.

Throughout the United States there is a scattering of groups and families, most often in rural areas, who care for their own dead without professional help. Some are coordinated by religious organizations, others by families or communities. "Nonprofessional Funerals," page 59 of this chapter, describes this in more detail. Chapter 7, "Death Ceremonies," gives complete instructions for organizing a memorial service.

In Canada there is a growing movement of cooperative mortuaries, mainly church led but not usually confined to church members. There are a few in the United States as well.

A church group in Arizona set up a "hot line" with a recording giving the prices charged by all the funeral directors in the area. Thousands of people have made use of this service.

Then too, many groups and individuals obtain reasonable prices for burial, cremation, and/or funeral services through careful shopping and negotiation before a death occurs. Memorial societies, described in Chapter 6, do this in over 200 communities in North America. Other ways of doing this are described in "Planning without a Society" and "Simplicity Without Pre-Planning" on pages 51 and 53–54 of this chapter.

Despite these options, the commercialization of funeral rites in Canada and the United States has resulted in expensive and often ostentatious funerals, at costs rising almost twice as fast as the cost of living. An estimated eight billion dollars is spent on funerals in the U.S. each year, not counting cemetery costs. In 1986 the average selling price of a "regular adult funeral" was $2,766, plus an average of $641 for such extras as vault, clothing and additional cars, and $395 for "cash advance" items (such as flowers and pallbearers) paid by the funeral director on behalf of the client, for a total of $3,802 average gross billing.[1] Average cemetery charges in excess of $1,200 were additional, bringing average costs for body disposition to around $5,000, the largest single purchase, after a house and car, for many consumers. Funeral costs have been rising almost twice as fast as the cost of living.

We heartily agree with funeral directors that death ceremonies, wisely planned, are important in meeting the social and emotional needs of survivors. See Chapter 7, "Death Ceremonies," We would add, however, that the amount of money spent on such ceremonies generally has little to do with how well they meet those needs. While families who want and can pay for expensive services should certainly have them, there are alternatives which are much less expensive and can meet the needs as well or better.

Why Are Most Funerals So Costly?

Funeral directing is an honorable and necessary business, but it is in a unique situation. About 22,000 funeral homes in the U.S. handle about two million deaths per year, an average of about ninety-one each. However, a tiny fraction of the funeral homes handle a majority of the business; thus many have less than one funeral per week. How do the thousands of morticians survive whose plants are idle more than eighty percent of the time?

Some have other sources of income. In the old days the "undertaker" usually ran a furniture store, and conducting funerals was a sideline related to the sale of merchandise he carried. Today, however, funeral directors who average as low as one funeral a week and have no other business must charge the overhead of days and weeks of idle plant to a single funeral. Only by charging exorbitant prices can these businesses survive. Such prices are possible because competition does not exist in this business in the same way it does in others.

Mark Twain puts it neatly in *Life on the Mississippi* with an undertaker saying:

> There's one thing in this world which a person don't say—
> "I'll look around a little and if I can't do better I'll come back
> and take it." That's a coffin. And take your poor man, and if
> you work him right he'll bust himself on a single layout. Or
> especially a woman.

Most bereaved relatives, in a state of shock and grief following a death, see no alternative to accepting what a funeral director presents as proper and acceptable. They, in turn, are naturally concerned as business people to sell sufficient services to meet expenses. This in itself is not illegal or unethical, but creates a serious problem for consumers.

Conglomerate ownership, both vertical and horizontal, is increasingly common in the funeral industry. For instance, the largest company in the funeral industry, Service Corporation International, as of 1989 operates 560 funeral homes, and 130 cemeteries. They also operate Provident Services, Inc. which finances funeral homes.

Regulation of the Funeral Industry

This situation in the funeral industry has naturally led to abuses, and these were dramatically brought to public attention in 1963 by Jessica Mitford's *The American Way of Death*. Even in 1983 the U.S. Senate Special Committee on Aging rated these abuses among the top ten most harmful frauds directed against the elderly.

In the U.S., the federal and state governments and the funeral industry itself have taken steps to curb these abuses and improve industry practices. The Federal Trade Commission, after years of study, public hearings and legal appeals by industry groups, approved a consumer protection rule requiring itemized price disclosures by funeral directors before arrangements are made, including price disclosure by telephone. Formerly common misrepresentations and unfair practices are forbidden.[2] However, surveys by local memorial societies and others have found widespread noncompliance with these rules. By law, the FTC must review the rule within four years to determine whether it should be changed or terminated. As we go to press, however, this review has not yet taken place. Individual states have additional consumer protection laws.

There is often confusion about state laws. Some funeral industry practices are required by law, some are not. Funeral directors are not always sure which are which and sometimes give incorrect information to clients. As one member of a regulatory board remarked, "Funeral directors are a goldmine of legal misinformation."

Laws regulating the funeral industry are based on the state's right to protect public health and safety. In many states, however, laws and regulations appear to have been drawn more in the interests of the funeral profession than of the public. For instance, while some states require embalming when a person has died from a contagious disease, the prevailing medical opinion is that no public health purpose is served by embalming.

It has been suggested that a "Truth in Death Services Act" would be helpful. This would be similar to the "Truth in Lending" and "Truth in Packaging" acts.

Funeral directors, like other business groups, have active lobbies in most state and provincial capitals. Most of the boards that regulate the funeral industry are composed of funeral directors. Regulations made by these boards acquire the force of law. Such regulations usually pertain to qualifications of funeral directors, funeral home requirements, etc., more than to consumer issues.

Consumer groups advocate that such regulatory bodies should instead contain a majority of non-industry members and provide full representation of the consumer viewpoint. It is important that memorial societies and other consumer organizations be alert to legislation affecting funeral practices and vigorously defend consumer interests. Consultation in such legislative efforts is available from the Continental Association of Funeral and Memorial Societies. See Appendix 6, "Directory of Memorial Societies."

Where to Go with Complaints

Complaints about funeral directors may be submitted to the Funeral Service Consumer Assistance Program carried on by the National Research and Information Center. See Appendix 2, "Organizations," for address and information.

Complaints concerning cemeteries may be referred to the Cemetery Consumer Service Council. See Appendix 2, "Organizations."

Complaints about burial monuments can be sent to Monument Builders of North America. See Appendix 2, "Organizations, for address and phone number."

AIDS and Funeral Directors

Consumer organizations have received many complaints about funeral homes refusing to handle bodies of persons who have died from acquired immunodeficiency syndrome (AIDS), or pressuring survivors who request burial to use cremation instead. In California and New York, advocacy groups have conducted surveys to identify funeral directors who will serve AIDS victims, and health departments and human rights agencies have checked on discriminatory practices by funeral directors. Airlines have also refused to transport bodies of AIDS victims, although normal requirements preclude any hazard. Health departments and the National Funeral Directors Association advise that bodies of AIDS victims may be safely handled using the precautions normally taken for the more contagious hepatitis B virus.

What Are the Options for Body Disposition?

The following options are listed in approximate order of cost, with the least expensive first. There is a great deal of variety within most of these options, which will be discussed later.

1. Immediate removal to a medical school, followed by a memorial service. If, at time of death, a body is accepted by a medical school, this generally involves no cost and performs a valuable service. Alternative plans should be made in case the body is not accepted. A few schools require the family to pay transportation. See Appendix 8, "Anatomical Gifts," for addresses and instructions on donations and alternate plans. There can be a brief gathering of the family before removal if circumstances permit, but this must be done quickly. See Chapter 7, "Death Ceremonies."
2. Immediate burial by the survivors without professional help. This may be done by the family, a religious group or a community group. It can be followed by a memorial service. See "Nonprofessional Funerals," page 59.
3. Immediate cremation, followed by a memorial service. Removal to the crematory can be handled by a funeral director or by family or friends. There may also be a committal service at the crematory chapel if desired, and/or later with the disposition of the ashes. See page 57 and 58, "About Cremation" and "Disposition of Ashes." Sample ceremonies are provided in Appendix 7, "Death Ceremonies."
4. Immediate burial handled by a funeral director, followed by a memorial service if desired. There may also be a graveside committal service if desired. Embalming is not required.
5. A funeral service in the presence of the body, followed by cremation or donation to a medical school. In this case embalming is usually chosen.
6. A funeral service in the presence of the body, followed by earth burial.

What's the Difference between Funeral and Memorial Services?

A funeral service is, by definition, a service held in the presence of the body. The casket may be open or closed. A memorial service is a service held after the body has been removed. Both serve the same purpose. Each has something to recommend it. A discussion of the two types of services will be found in Chapter 7, "Death Ceremonies."

The Practice of Simplicity

Simplicity in arrangements can effect great economy, but even more importantly it can help center attention on spiritual values and the life of the person who has died, rather than on material things. It can avoid the appearance of ostentation and extravagance. Removal of the body within twenty-four hours, followed by a memorial service, allows the ceremony to focus on the life of the one who has died, with the healing which that can bring.

Family Participation

Family members can be helped to recognize and accept a death, and begin the process of grieving, by helping in the removal and disposition of the body. It is often good for the closest family members to be given an opportunity to accompany the body to its destination and to help load and unload it. If burial is used, they may accompany the body to the graveside and start the filling of the grave. Family or friends may have a suitable vehicle, such as a station wagon, van or pickup truck, for conveying the body, and a family member should be encouraged to drive it. A hearse is not required. The length of the box for transporting a body should be considered in choosing a vehicle for transportation.

There may be a brief committal service at the graveside or crematory. This may include a prayer, poem or song, as desired. Chapter 7, Death Ceremonies, contains many suggestions for meaningful participation in funerals and memorial services by family and friends.

The Need for Planning

Simplicity doesn't happen by accident. When death occurs in a family in which there was no planning, the survivors find themselves virtually helpless in the face of entrenched custom, dealing with a funeral director who expects them to follow this custom. Through planning, however, family members can have the precedent, information and moral support needed to get the type of service they want.

Thousands of Families Being Helped

To help with advance planning, nonprofit funeral and memorial societies have been formed in some two hundred cities in the United States and Canada with a membership of over one million. These societies cooperate with funeral directors, sometimes by having contracts with them and sometimes by advising their members as to which firms provide the desired services. They also assist those who wish to leave their bodies for education or their eyes or other tissues for transplant or therapy. See Chapter 6, "Memorial Societies."

If No Memorial Society Is Near

How near must a society be? Some societies cover just one town. Some have connections with, or information on, funeral directors in several states. Much depends on the kind of services wanted. It may be economical to use a funeral director or crematory quite far away if the body needs to be transported only one way, as when a memorial service is used. In the United States, if there is not a memorial society near enough to help, contact the Continental Association of Funeral and Memorial Societies, 7910 Woodmont Ave., Suite 1208, Bethesda MD 20814-3015. See Appendix 6, "Directory of Memorial Societies."

Planning without a Society

The simple arrangements and low rates obtained through a memorial society may sometimes be obtained by individual arrangement, though this is likely to be difficult. Sometimes a church, labor or fraternal group can find a cooperative funeral director and make such arrangements on behalf of its members. In such cases it is good to keep participation open to nonmembers and to look forward to becoming a full-fledged memorial society.

The family should talk the matter over, preferably while all are in good health, and decide whether cremation, burial or medical school is preferred, whether there shall be viewing of the remains, and whether a funeral or memorial service is wanted. These are the main decisions. Then call or visit various funeral directors, explaining your wishes, and see what each has to offer.

National Coalition for Fair Funeral Prices

A recent and highly encouraging development for the benefit of those seeking reasonable funeral costs is the National Coalition for Fair Funeral Prices. It originated with a local Interfaith Funeral Information

Committee in Phoenix, Arizona. Research by this committee indicated that many mortuaries and pre-need plans overcharge by $500 to $3,000 per funeral, while complete funerals, including a metal casket, are available in many communities for $800 or less.

The Coalition has placed advertisements in local and national publications listing fair funeral prices and offering detailed instructions to assist local groups in setting up information services. As part of this assistance they offer to supply wholesale price lists of caskets so that consumers can tell if they are being overcharged by mortuaries.

Detailed information about the Coalition will be found in Appendix 5, "Simple Burial."

Local Surveys of Funeral Costs

In several places, the local newspaper or broadcasting station has made a survey of funeral costs. These have produced phenomenal public response.

Sometimes these surveys are made by the newspaper or broadcasting station itself and sometimes they are made in cooperation with the Better Business Bureau or with a memorial society, a civic organization, a church or a group of churches.

For suggestions on how to conduct such a survey, contact the National Coalition, or the Continental Associaton of Funeral & Memorial Societies (See Appendices 2 and 6). They can supply excellent material, including video tapes for television use.

Planning Helps Understanding

Advance planning is needed, not only in making arrangements with funeral directors, but for working out understanding within the family. A young man killed in an accident left a widow and young children with no savings. Both husband and wife believed in simple burial, and the widow was fortunate in getting a funeral director who encouraged her to carry out her desire for a simple and economical arrangement. The young man's mother, however, though unable to help with the expenses, insisted on an elaborate funeral. Since there had been no advance planning, the wife was unable to resist and not only had to endure a ceremony distressing to her, but had to face life with small children, her husband gone, and a heavy funeral debt hanging over her. More explicit planning might have avoided this unhappy outcome.

Persons wishing to leave organs or tissues to aid the living, or who wish to leave their bodies to a medical school, have a particular responsibility to reach an understanding with their families ahead of time.

If a family is not in agreement about body disposition, the surviving spouse, or other survivor if there is no spouse, has the legal right to make the decision in most states. A lawyer should be consulted if a person wishes to make plans or arrangements binding on survivors.

Write It Down!

A valuable help in planning is a four-page form called "Putting My House in Order," which is available from the Continental Association of Funeral & Memorial Societies. See Appendix 6, "Directory of Memorial Societies." Plans for body disposition and death ceremonies, as well as financial and property records, can be indicated on this form. Similar, though less detailed forms are available from the NFDA and several cemetery associations. See Appendix 2, "Organizations." Do *not* include funeral plans in your will, as wills are seldom read until after the funeral.

Simplicity Without Pre-Planning

If you desire simplicity and economy but are confronted with a death in the family without advance plans, there are still alternatives, though not as easy. First of all, consider the options listed on page 49 of this chapter.

If you opt for immediate removal to a medical school, consult the Directory of Medical Schools in Appendix 8 to determine which, if any, medical schools within a reasonable radius are in need of bodies, then phone the Anatomy Department there to see if the body may be accepted.

If you prefer some other alternative, check to see if there is a memorial society in your area. See Appendix 6, "Directory of Memorial Societies." Call the society. It may be too late to join, but, in any case, the volunteer will give you as much advice, moral support and information as possible. Some societies will accept members at this time.

If this can't be arranged, ask some knowledgeable friend, perhaps your clergyman, to help you locate a cooperative funeral director. The 1984 Federal Trade Commission (FTC) rule requires funeral directors to provide price information over the phone on request, as well as in person. *Be sure* your friend goes with you to see the funeral director and help make arrangements. Your friend can ask questions without embarrassment and can give important moral support.

Bear in mind that funeral directors are often skilled merchandisers who downplay their cheaper merchandise. Don't be put off if the funeral director refers to a simple service as a "welfare funeral." An itemized price list of services and merchandise must be presented, whether requested or not, before arrangements are made, under the FTC rule.

While funeral "packages" are still offered, you are no longer required to accept this, and items deleted must be deducted from the cost charged.

If you prefer to make your own burial box, find a funeral director who is willing to handle this, rather than selling his or her own merchandise. Some funeral directors will also rent caskets, if viewing is desired but will be followed by cremation rather than burial. The key is shopping around, preferably in advance.

Financial Resources at Time of Death

Social Security Death Benefits. A Social Security lump sum death payment of $255 is available in some cases to survivors of covered workers. This benefit must be formally applied for. Those eligible are:

1. A surviving spouse living with the covered worker at time of death. This includes a spouse separated *solely* for medical reasons, such as residence in a hospital or nursing home.
2. A surviving spouse *not* living with the covered worker at the time of death is eligible for the payment only if she or he was receiving a monthly benefit as a spouse during the month of death or would have been eligible for such benefit if an application had been filed for it.
3. If there is no surviving eligible spouse, a child will be eligible for the lump sum payment if he or she was eligible for Social Security monthly benefits on the deceased's record during the month of death of the covered worker.

Union and Fraternal Benefits are provided by many trade union and fraternal organizations to the families of their members. Many such benefits go unclaimed because families are unaware of them. Also, there are benefits for the survivors of any man who has ever been a railroad employee. Some of these benefits are available only for funeral expenses.

Insurance and Employee Benefits. No family needs to be told to file claims for life insurance. Often, however, there are other forms of insurance, depending on the circumstances of the death, which provide benefits for the survivors. If occupational factors were involved in the death, Workman's Compensation Insurance may be in effect. There may be automobile club insurance. In other cases liability insurance of one kind or another may be invoked. The families of state employees in some states are entitled to survivor benefits. Such possibilities should be checked. Burial expenses for indigent families are commonly paid by the county.

Benefits for Veterans. The Veterans Administration (VA) will pay a $300 burial and funeral allowance for those who were, at time of death, entitled to receive pension or compensation or would have been entitled but for receipt of military retired pay, or if death occurs in a VA facility or a contract nursing home to which the deceased was properly admitted. Some transportation costs may also be paid.

Veterans who die of a service-connected disability are eligible for up to $1,100 burial allowance in lieu of other burial benefits.

A veteran can be buried in a National Cemetery (transportation costs paid under certain circumstances) and receive a government headstone or marker for a grave in a government or other cemetery. Some national cemeteries also have grave sites, garden niches or columbaria available for cremated remains. In lieu of burial in a government cemetery, a $150 plot allowance will be made. An allowance toward the purchase of a marker in lieu of a government headstone/marker is available, in the amount of $71 as of October 1, 1985.

Families of veterans also may be eligible for ongoing financial assistance in the form of monthly survivor benefits. Your local Social Security and Veterans Administration offices and your funeral director can assist you in obtaining these benefits. Be prepared for a lengthy process. Red tape can take a long time.

Protection through a Credit Union.   Many, but not all, credit unions have an arrangement whereby deposits made before age fifty-five are doubled (not to exceed $1,000 or $2,000) at time of death. In most credit unions, however, if death occurs between fifty-five and sixty, 75% of savings are matched; between sixty and sixty-five, 50%; between sixty-five and seventy, 25%; and after seventy, none.

Thus a person under fifty-five, by making a savings deposit of $500, creates a death benefit fund of $1,000 but still receives interest on the $500 savings and can withdraw them at any time.

Another arrangement is to borrow the $500 from the credit union and deposit it as savings, thus (for a person fifty-five and under) creating a $1,000 death benefit fund. When the loan is paid, interest will accrue on the savings. If the loan is not paid, it will be cancelled by the credit union at time of death.

Either of the above arrangements is an entirely legitimate and businesslike way of covering burial expenses for any member of the family. But check first with your credit union to make sure they offer the desired services.

Life Insurance.   Many families carry a small insurance policy on each member for the specific purpose of meeting burial expense in case of death. In such cases, the family should decide in advance what types of services are wanted and what they are likely to cost. Otherwise the expense may be several times the anticipated amount. Just as inflation makes life insurance a poor form of savings, so it makes it a costly way to provide for death expenses — though better than none.

Mutual Aid Plans.   Some groups, including a number of Mennonite Church congregations, assess each family when a death occurs.

A *"Totten Trust"*   is a savings account in your name to which is added "in trust for..." the relative or friend who is to use the funds as you direct. It may be in a credit union, bank or other savings institution. Be sure to check the interest rate, however, as it may be relatively low.

Prepaid Funeral Arrangements

Much promotion has recently gone into the selling of prepaid funeral contracts. A million or more are being sold each year at a cost of billions of dollars. All too often the selling of these arrangements provides an occasion for "upgrading" the funeral (making it more expensive).

In general, a consumer can get the same security and benefits by placing the funds in a savings account or trust for funeral purposes, a credit union, or other conservative investment. Such funds remain under the control of the consumer and can be transferred to another location or institution without penalty. They can be changed if desired, or withdrawn, complete with accumulated interest.

Although most states have some type of legislation governing pre-need sales, these laws have not been adequate to prevent a striking increase in complaints from consumers alleging deceptive marketing and difficulty in obtaining refunds when moving or cancelling a contract. In response, the American Association of Retired Persons, Continental Association of Funeral and Memorial Societies, and Consumer Federation of America in 1987 prepared "A Model Law for Prepaid Funeral Arrangements," incorporating necessary consumer protections.

Useful precautions include:

1. Deal only with an established and reputable company. Check with the Better Business Bureau, Attorney General's Office, etc., to be sure.
2. Consider only a guaranteed price plan in which there can be no additional costs or price changes.
3. Accept only a plan which places 90% of prepaid funds in trust, and only if there is adequate state protection for trusted funds. An attorney's advice will be worthwhile in determining this.
4. Be sure the contract allows the right of cancellation, with refund of trusted monies, plus interest earnings remaining after deduction for fees, expenses and taxes. An added protection is the right of cancellation within the first 30 days with full refund of monies paid. Some state laws mandate 72 hours in which any contract purchased at home may be cancelled.
5. The Continental Association of Funeral and Memorial Societies and the American Association of Retired Persons suggest consulting a lawyer before signing any pre-need contract.

About Cremation

Modern cremation is a process for returning a body to the elements through intense heat and evaporation. It is completed in one to three hours and results in three to seven pounds of small clean white bone fragments, usually called "ashes", or cremated remains. Crematories can pulverize these fragments if desired. For reasons of aesthetics and economy the use of cremation is increasing rapidly in the United States, rising from 7.66% of deaths in 1974 to 13.87% in 1985. In Canada the rate in 1985 was 25.84%, while 85% of those who die in England are cremated.

Cremation is an ancient practice, dating back at least to Biblical times, when Saul and his sons were cremated, as recorded in the book of I Samuel 31. It has been practiced for thousands of years by Hindus and Buddhists, and was common in England from 787 A.D. Most religious groups, including the Roman Catholic Church, now permit cremation without question. The Greek Orthodox Church and Conservative and Orthodox Jews oppose it, as do some conservative Protestant groups, Moslems, and Baha'is.

Crematory charges average around $150 (with the exception of Alaska) for the cremation itself, plus cost of a rigid, combustible and covered container. Many crematories and funeral directors can provide fiberboard body containers, at a cost of from $10 to $125. Some charge extra for mailing of cremated remains. *Caring for Your Own Dead*, by Lisa Carlson, lists crematories in most states that will accept a body directly from a family, and gives prices charged. Massachusetts, Michigan, Nebraska, New Hampshire and New Jersey are not listed because state regulations require that funeral directors must handle these arrangements. See Appendix 1, "Bibliography."

Cremation normally costs less than earth burial if arrangements are made directly by the family or through a funeral director who works with a memorial society. However, the funeral director's charges for transportation and paper work are often more than the cost of cremation itself. A full fledged funeral in the presence of the body may bring the cost of cremation into the same range as the cost of earth burial. A memorial service, held after the body has been removed, as I explain in Chapter 7, "Death Ceremonies," not only saves expense but focuses attention on the life of the person instead of on the dead body.

For Profit Cremation Services

In recent years private companies in many areas have offered the service of immediate body removal and cremation, without embalming, sometimes (but not always!) at low cost. Some states have a special license for such "direct disposers." Some cremation services call themselves "societies," apparently taking advantage of the good reputation of memorial societies, although they are actually private businesses. These can be helpful services for those in areas not served by memorial societies. Where there is a memorial society, however, membership offers added information, options, and flexibility, as well as supporting the consumer voice in the funeral industry.

Disposition of Ashes

Cremation remains, are clean and white and can be stored indefinitely. The crematory places them in temporary containers of cardboard, tin, or plastic, in which they may be mailed by registered mail and some express services (but not by United Parcel Service). Some families prefer to scatter them in a favorite garden or woods, from a mountain top, or at sea. First be sure they are pulverized, to avoid visible bone fragments. Only California places restrictions on disposition of cremated remains. In California, the remains may be scattered at sea, interred in a cemetery, or kept at home. Cremated remains may also be stored in a special container called an urn.

Many church burial grounds and commercial cemeteries provide space for disposition of cremated remains. Some provide for scattering, some for earth burial, and some for placement in a columbarium (a structure containing niches for a number of urns). Memorial gardens are becoming increasing popular — cemeteries in which markers, if any, are level with the ground, providing a more parklike setting. If you are considering such a disposition, take time to compare options and prices, as costs vary greatly.

Earth Burial

Earth burial is still the most common form of body disposition in the United States and Canada. Burial may be in commercial cemeteries, church cemeteries, or (in some states) family burying grounds or individually owned land. "Traditional" cemeteries allow families to select any gravestone they like. "Memorial parks" require that stones be level with the ground.

Prices for grave plots vary from about $150 to $600 or more. Opening and closing a grave costs a minimum of $300, with an extra charge for weekends or holidays. Concrete grave liners are required by most cemeteries to prevent the ground above the grave from sinking with time. Concrete or metal vaults may also be used as grave liners; some are guaranteed waterproof for a period of years and costs range up to $2,000 and more. Some of these are sold with the erroneous claim that they will preserve the body. Some people choosing earth burial prefer that their bodies return to the earth in a natural manner, and therefore use wood or corrugated boxes. Simple grave markers cost a minimum of $250 plus engraving.

Transporting of Bodies

Sometimes a body needs to be transported for a ceremony or interment in a distant place. If a common carrier is to be used, a funeral director will be required and will know what to do. Before using air express, check with AMTRAK. It offers quick service to many destinations and is much cheaper than air. Never move a body without a permit or medical permission.

Handling of transportation by members of the family can be both emotionally wholesome and economical. If the body is to be transported by the family in a suitable vehicle, a death certificate and transportation permit must be obtained according to local regulations. County registrars, health departments, coroners, and funeral directors can provide information on regulations. Lisa Carlson's *Caring For Your Own Dead* provides detailed, state-by-state information on regulations and procedures. See Appendix 1, "Bibliography." All states honor the proper permits from other states when a body is moved. Depending on the weather and the distance to be traveled, embalming or dry ice may be needed. There may be local regulations which necessitate such measures as embalming or hermetic sealing of the casket. This can be talked over with the Health Department.

Nonprofessional Funerals

Some groups and individuals care for their own dead without the assistance of a funeral director. A few are religious groups such as the Quakers or Mennonites. Others are rural families, particularly in Appalachia. Some are organized within the framework of a memorial society. Each operates within the laws of its own state, which vary widely.

While individuals can successfully care for their dead in many areas, it is highly desirable for families who wish to do this to join forces with other members of their church or local community. Moral support is an important factor. The first time the Burial Committee of the Yellow Springs (Ohio) Friends Meeting had occasion to care for one of their dead, we received a sharp response from the funeral directors who, together with a representative of the state board, descended upon us. Fortunately our group contained several substantial citizens and had carefully researched the matter in advance. We explained to our visitors our philosophy and the laws of Ohio, whereupon they smiled and politely went away. This would have been more difficult for a single family. Since that time, using this as a precedent, some individual families have cared for their own dead without group assistance.

Requirements vary from state to state, and crematories and cemeteries may have rules of their own. These laws and regulations — generally public health statutes and regulations governing licensing and operations of funeral directors, cemeteries and crematories — must be carefully checked. Information for all states is provided in Carlson's *Caring For Your Own Dead*. She has found that the only states *requiring* disposition by a funeral director are Massachusetts, Michigan, Nebraska, New Hampshire, and New Jersey. New York and Louisiana are relatively restrictive, but a family may transport the body. She attributes these limitations to funeral director lobbying, combined with lack of information to legislators.

For instructions on building inexpensive burial boxes, see Appendix 5, "Simple Burial."

An Example

The Burial Committee of the Yellow Springs Friends Meeting has functioned successfully for many years. Member families fill out forms in advance, authorizing the committee to act on their behalf, and include the necessary biographical data and endorsement by the next-of-kin. The form is shown in Appendix 5, "Simple Burial."

When a death occurs, a member of the committee gets the death certificate signed by the attending physician or coroner and takes it to the health department to be recorded. The committee keeps blank death certificate forms on hand. The next of kin signs an "authorization to cremate" and makes out a check to the crematory. Burial or removal to a medical school follows much the same pattern. Committee members serve without pay, which minimizes the possibility of legal complications.

At the same time that the disposition of the body is being handled, committee members assist the family with food, baby sitting, hospitality for relatives, getting out death notices, etc., and helping to plan a suitable memorial service. This support is very meaningful.

This committee and its arrangements did not come into being overnight. The committee had examined the laws and explained their plans carefully to the state and local departments of health. They set up advance arrangements with a crematory and visited each of the nearby hospitals so that there would be no misunderstanding or delay when a death occurred.

An example of a simple, nonprofessional burial was the occasion of my wife's death. The burial committee of the Celo (NC) Friends Meeting quietly functioned. Friends and students at the Arthur Morgan School quickly built a box from materials already at hand and cut to size. They dug a grave in the Friends' Burial Ground, arranged a graveside committal service followed later by a memorial service, and assisted the family in various other ways. The whole thing was beautifully handled, conveying a warm feeling of fellowship and support. My total cash expense was $23 for plywood plus a $2 filing fee.

The Coroner's Role

It is important to understand the role of the coroner if there is one in your county. His responsibility is to check on accidental deaths, homicides, suicides and sudden or unexpected deaths, especially when no physician has been in attendance. It is mandatory that all such deaths be reported to him promptly. It is his job to determine the cause of death and whether there has been foul play. He should be given active cooperation. A friend of mine, a Christian Scientist, died without benefit of a physician. His family wished to handle arrangements without a funeral director but didn't realize they needed a death certificate from the coroner. This got them into some embarrassing difficulty which, fortunately, the Yellow Springs Friends Meeting Burial Committee was able to resolve.

Death in a Foreign Country

Some 8,000 Americans die in foreign countries each year. Everyone going abroad should carry in their passports instructions to be followed in the event of death. This should be done regardless of age or good health and discussed with families before leaving, to avoid conflicting instructions. A second choice should be indicated in case the first is not available. The full name of father, maiden name of mother, full (maiden) name of spouse, date and place of birth, and occupation should be listed. The exact location of any will should be included, along with the name of the executor, if any.

If someone dies abroad while accompanied by an adult member of the immediate family, that family member will make the arrangements. The nearest American consular office should be contacted and can give advice. If no adult family member is along, the consular office is responsible to notify the next of kin in the United States and then carry out their instructions concerning disposition of the body. The consul will furnish a "report of death" which has the legal status of a death certificate. The consul is also prepared to serve as "provisional conservator" (not administrator) of the deceased's property in the foreign country. A small percentage fee is charged for this.

Advance payment in full is normally required for disposition of the body. If instructions and/or payment is not received in a reasonable length of time, the consular office allows local authorities to dispose of the body as unclaimed.

Cremation, in countries with facilities for it, is normally the least expensive method of disposition. If cremation is not available in the country where death occurred, it may be available in a nearby country. Costs vary greatly. In the Sudan a cremation costs $60, in France, $1,500. Ashes may, if desired, be sent home by mail. Earth burial is universally available and varies greatly in cost. In some countries it may be cheaper than cremation.

Often bodies of people who die abroad are flown home. This requires embalming, which is not always readily available, plus special packing and a hermetically sealed coffin plus an outside shipping case. This adds up to several thousand dollars. Consulates usually know which mortuaries are able to handle such complex shipments. It will normally be less costly to dispose of the body without shipping it home. If you prefer the cheapest way, be sure to say so. Don't hesitate to "shop around."

What To Do when Death Occurs, if a Funeral Director Is Used

A doctor or coroner must declare the person dead and sign a death certificate, which can be obtained from the hospital, health department or funeral director.

When family members are ready to have the body taken away, the funeral director of their choice is called. See Chapter 2, "Living with Dying." The hospital or nursing home will do this for you if the death has occurred there. Memorial society members will call a funeral director who has a contract with or is recommended by their society. A clergyman, appropriate church or synagogue committee, or friend should be contacted promptly to help where necessary, and especially in making arrangements with the funeral director if there has been no advance planning. See pages 53–54.

Checklist of Things To Be Done

(You may wish to tear out or photocopy these pages and attach them to your plans for final arrangements.)

☐ Arrange for members of family or friends to take turns answering door or phone, keeping careful record of calls.
☐ Coordinate the supplying of food for the next days.
☐ Arrange appropriate child care.
☐ Decide on time and place of funeral or memorial service(s). See Chapter 7, "Death Ceremonies," pages 127–145.

- [ ] If flowers are to be omitted, decide on appropriate memorial to which gifts may be made (such as a church, library, school or charity).
- [ ] Make list of immediate family, close friends and employer or business colleagues. Notify each by phone.
- [ ] Prepare list of distant persons to be notified by letter and/or printed notice, and decide which to send each.
- [ ] Write obituary. Check cost with newspaper. Some newspapers charge as much as $200 and more for death notices. In this case, a written notice may be mailed to friends. If you submit a death notice to the paper, include age, place of birth, cause of death, occupation, college degree(s), memberships held, military service, outstanding work, and list of survivors in immediate family. Give time and place of services. Deliver in person or by phone to newspapers.
- [ ] Arrange for hospitality for visiting relatives and friends.
- [ ] Consider special needs of the household, for cleaning, etc., which might be done by friends.
- [ ] Select pallbearers and notify them. See Chapter 7, "Death Ceremonies," page 71.
- [ ] If deceased was living alone, notify utilities and landlord and tell post office where to send mail. Take precaution against thieves, especially during the time of the funeral/memorial service.
- [ ] Plan for disposition of flowers after funeral (e.g., hospital or rest home).
- [ ] Prepare list of persons to receive acknowledgments of flowers, calls, food, etc. Send appropriate acknowledgments. (Can be written notes, printed acknowledgments or some of each.)
- [ ] Notify lawyer and executor. Get several copies of death certificate.
- [ ] Check carefully all life and casualty insurance and death benefits, including Social Security, credit union, trade union, fraternal, military, etc. Check also on income for survivors from these sources.
- [ ] Check promptly on all debts and installment payments. Some may carry insurance clauses that will cancel them. If there is to be a delay in meeting payments, consult with creditors and ask for more time before the payments are due.

Planning for Inheritance—Keeping Down Legal Costs

Survivorship can be enormously simplified if the person who has died has taken the trouble to discuss these financial matters with his or her family and make appropriate plans. Failure to do so can lead to conflict and much unnecessary work and expense.

Everyone who owns property should make a will, carefully determining what he or she wants to do and paying a competent attorney to draw up the document. If a person dies without a will, his or her property will be distributed in accordance with state law, often not at all what the person would have chosen. An executor to administer the estate also should be selected in advance. If not provided in the will, an executor will be appointed by the court. Since each state has its own rules concerning wills, a will needs to be reviewed, and perhaps redrawn, if a person moves to a new state.

Careful estate planning may also minimize state and federal inheritance taxes and probate costs. There are many legal instruments for doing this, and tax laws frequently change. It is therefore advisable to consult an attorney to make one's plans.

Probate

Probate is a court proceeding to verify a will and clear title to property being inherited through a will or under the law of intestacy. Probate proceedings provide an orderly inheritance process, but may be very costly and time consuming (often at least a year).

Former U.S. Chief Justice Warren Burger once commented that standard legal fees charged to probate an estate after a death are frequently out of proportion to the value of the services rendered. These fees are in some cases well earned; in others they constitute a sheer windfall. Justice Burger remarked that the legal profession had allowed the "relatively simple business" of settling a will to "become encrusted with excess procedure baggage that ... often adds unreasonably to costs." Often a percentage of the value of the estate is charged, regardless of the amount of work involved. A helpful book is Norman F. Dacey's *How To Avoid Probate—Updated*. See Appendix 1, "Bibliography- —Simple Burial."

While it is wise to use an attorney in these matters, a family may minimize legal fees by handling many of the details that usually take up much of the attorney's time, using the attorney in an advisory capacity and to handle the more technical matters. All records concerning finances, property, insurance, etc., should be kept in good order and readily accessible, as attorneys often spend much expensive time straightening out records. See "Write It Down!" page 53. It is entirely proper to negotiate with an attorney to pay only for the actual time spent. At present, $50–$75 an hour is not unreasonable. Better yet, arrange a flat fee for the job. Sometimes an experienced accountant can handle the entire process. For such work, especially if the accountant is a CPA, she or he should receive a comparable rate of pay.

Choosing a lawyer at a time of grieving can be stressful. To avoid this, it may be helpful to discuss periodically with a spouse which local lawyers seem to be good ones.

Beware of Vultures

Survivors, particularly widows, are commonly preyed upon by swindlers of one kind or another. A favorite device is to collect a nonexistent debt owed by the deceased, or to deliver merchandise (commonly a Bible) that was never ordered.

Another ploy is to inform the survivor of a nonexistent life insurance policy on which a final premium must be paid before benefits can be collected, or of some other valuable asset requiring a final payment of some kind. Widows are prime prospects for bad investments and even reputable investment firms, when asked, will sometimes recommend changing stock portfolios merely for the sake of the commissions involved.

The moral is: be careful, go slow and consult an experienced member of the family or other trusted business advisor.

REFERENCES

[1]Federated Funeral Directors of America, Springfield, Illinois. Federated Funeral Directors performs accounting services for approximately 1,300 funeral homes from New York State to the Dakotas.

[2]Federal Trade Commission, "Funeral Industry Practices: Trade Regulation Rule," *Federal Register*, 47:186, and in *Code of Federal Regulations*, 16 CFR Ch.1, Part 453, Funeral Industry Practices.

6   MEMORIAL SOCIETIES

No discussion of death education, of hospice, or of simple burial can be considered comprehensive which does not include a report on memorial societies. Memorial societies constitute the most important lay movement of our time relating to funeral practices and death ceremonies. A directory of funeral and memorial societies in the U.S. and Canada will be found in Appendix 6, "Directory of Memorial Societies."

As author of A Manual of Simple Burial, I was invited in 1963 to attend the founding meeting of the Continental Association of Funeral and Memorial Societies and served for many years on its board of directors. The Manual has served as source book and advocate for the memorial society movement since its inception. My daughter, Jenifer Morgan, who has collaborated in recent editions, is a former Executive Secretary of the Continental Association.

What They Are and How They Work

Memorial societies are cooperative, nonprofit consumer organizations, democratically run, that help their members to get simplicity, dignity and economy in funeral arrangements through advance planning. They are not run by funeral directors.

These societies themselves generally do not offer funeral services but act in an advisory capacity and often have contracts or agreements with funeral directors on behalf of their members. Thus they help their members to get exactly the services they want, and at reasonable cost. The work of the societies is done by unpaid volunteers in most societies; a few of the larger societies have paid secretaries.

Memorial societies do collectively what few individual families are prepared to do — they inquire around, compare services and prices, then share this information with their members. They do *not* collect payment for funeral services. For information on alternatives for the disposition of bodies, see Chapter 5, "Simple Burial and Cremation."

There are memorial societies in about 190 cities in North America, with a combined membership of about one half million. Most societies charge a onetime membership fee of $10 to $30, and some have a small Records Charge, which they collect from the family at time of death, via the funeral director. A few have a small annual membership fee. They effect large savings for their members and are an outstanding example of how consumers, by democratic group effort, can empower themselves at the grassroots level.

Memorial Services

In addition to advising their members on funeral arrangements, these societies can often help with suggestions for memorial services. See also Chapter 7, "Death Ceremonies."

Membership Is Transferable

Families moving to another city can transfer their membership at little or no charge. Likewise when a death occurs away from home, the society in the host city, and its cooperating funeral director, will assist the family.

History

The practice of group planning for funeral arrangements started early in the century in the Farm Grange organization in the northwestern United States. From there the idea spread to the cities, mainly under church leadership. The People's Memorial Association of Seattle, organized in 1939, was the first urban group. Organizations spread gradually up and down the West Coast, then eastward across the United States and again northward into Canada.

Continental Association of Funeral and Memorial Societies

By 1963 the societies had become a strong continent-wide movement, and the Cooperative League of the U.S.A. called a meeting in Chicago, where Canadian and U.S. societies together formed the Continental Association. The member societies, and literature available from the Association, are listed in Appendix 6, "Directory of Memorial Societies." The Association serves as a central clearinghouse for information and publicity and assists new societies in forming. In several states where there are a number of societies, state federations have been organized to follow consumer issues within the state and to act as needed.

Having a strong central office, the Association is the principal advocate for the consumer of funeral services. In this capacity it speaks not only for its immediate membership but for the 247 million Americans who are not members, all of whom must someday die. Working closely with the Federal Trade Commission, it was instrumental in securing passage — after a long struggle — of legislation requiring funeral directors to quote prices freely and to offer their services on an itemized basis, rather than as package deals. (A review of this law is currently pending.) This does not tell people what kind of funerals they should have, but broadens their opportunity for choice and opens up important savings.

The Memorial Society Association of Canada

In 1971 the Canadian Association was formed, in close collaboration with the Continental Association. It performs in Canada essentially the same functions as those performed by the Continental Association in the U.S. Together the two associations include nearly all the bona fide memorial societies in North America. See Appendix 6, "Directory of Memorial Societies," for the names and addresses. (As we go to press the Canadian Association is in process of reorganization.)

How to Organize a Memorial Society

An organizational *Handbook for Funeral and Memorial Societies* is available for $10.00 from the Continental Association. In addition, the Association has area coordinators, persons experienced in memorial society organization, who are located in various parts of the country and are often able to give a hand in helping new societies to get started.

Financial Savings

Memorial society members commonly save fifty to seventy-five percent of usual funeral costs, with total savings to members of millions of dollars annually. In 1990 the People's Memorial Association of Seattle, the largest society in the U.S., had a contract for funeral service and burial at $625, to be compared with an average cost for an adult funeral of $3,500. Cemetery costs commonly bring the total to $5,000 or more. For the ninety-five percent of PMA members electing cremation, the contracted price is $395. An average of about 1,300 services are provided to PMA members annually, helping to make funeral costs on the West Coast the lowest in the U.S. These savings resulted in part from collective bargaining but more from the simplicity that members are encouraged to practice.

Cooperation with Funeral Directors

In many cases, memorial societies negotiate contracts or agreements with funeral directors through which the society members can get the services they desire, and at predetermined prices. While funeral directors originally took a dim view of memorial societies, arrangements between funeral directors and societies generally have proved satisfactory to all concerned.

In cases where no contracts or agreements can be arranged, memorial societies are generally able to advise their members where to turn to get the services and prices they want. In a couple of cases where funeral directors refused to cooperate at all, the societies found ways to bypass them altogether.

The Social Base of Memorial Societies

By and large it has been prosperous, educated, middle-class families that have organized memorial societies — doctors, lawyers, teachers, business people. Mostly they have been church people, too, and mainly concerned with simplicity. Ironically, working-class families and minority ethnic groups, on whom the burden of funeral costs falls most heavily, have been less inclined to join memorial societies.

Memorial society leaders have been concerned with this and have kept the doors of membership open to all. Some societies actively seek members and leadership from minority groups and the less affluent, with modest success in recent years.

Imitation "Societies"

The success and popularity of memorial societies have led to imitations. Private companies, calling themselves societies, have entered the funeral service business in various places. Some offer "direct cremation" service. This is a valid form of disposition of human remains, but it is misleading for such firms to call themselves "societies."

If someone from a "society" tries to sell you something or offers you a prepayment plan, investigate carefully. Memorial societies have no commercial interests and rarely charge membership fees over $30. In general, memorial societies advise against prepayment plans. There are various ways to make advance financial provision for death. See Chapter 5, "Simple Burial and Cremation," pages 54–56.

Nearly all bona fide societies in the United States are members of the Continental Association. When in doubt about a society, check in the directory in Appendix 6, "Directory of Memorial Societies," to see if it is a member, or contact CAFMS.

7 DEATH CEREMONIES

I heartily agree with funeral directors that ceremonies at a time of death are important in meeting the social and emotional needs of survivors. This chapter presents the viewpoint, however, that effective and appropriate ceremonies are possible with very little expense. And that conversely, elaborate and expensive ceremonies may distract attention from the meaning and value of the life of the one who has died.

The chapter includes detailed instruction on many aspects of death ceremonies, particularly encouraging participation of family and friends in whatever type of service is chosen. Appendix 7, "Sample Death Ceremonies," includes sample ceremonies and readings which may be used.

Much of the work of preparing this chapter was done by Ann Baty, of the Bowling Green Memorial Society, who studied the subject over a period of years and corresponded with hundreds of clergy and lay people. Valuable ideas were derived also from Dr. Leroy Bowman's The American Funeral, which remains an authoritative source after thirty-five years, and from my own experience.

Humankind, from earliest times, has practiced death ceremonies and procedures in great variety. The reason for these ceremonies is not hard to understand. Such procedures are important to the healing process. No human being lives in a social vacuum; our speech, habits, values — the very meaning of life — derive from our association with one another. Hence the death of one individual is traumatic for the survivors. Recognizing that death ceremonies and related customs are important in meeting the social and emotional needs of survivors, we should plan these ceremonies carefully.

In recent years there has been a worldwide move towards deritualized funerals (and other ceremonies, too). Our purpose in this section of the *Manual* is not to weaken or eliminate ritual but to help create more meaningful rituals.

Needs to Be Met by Death Ceremonies

Every situation is different, with different circumstances, different personalities and different needs. Here are some of the needs that are commonly found, and ways in which appropriate ceremonies can help meet them.

Reestablishing Relationships. Death, like marriage, changes a broad range of relationships, as between parent and child, brother and sister, and friends. After a death in the family we are not quite the same people we were before. We therefore must rediscover ourselves in a new set of relationships. This relates directly to the process of mourning.

A promising child of a prominent family had died suddenly, to the great shock of the family and community. A simple service had been held, with just the family and a few close friends. Then for days afterwards, as the mother encountered other good friends, each felt the necessity of conveying sympathy, at the expense of unhappiness to themselves and of rubbing fresh salt in the wounds of the mother.

Had the service been open to all, in quarters large enough to receive the friends, the individual condolences could have been replaced by a single meeting, the relationships reestablished, and life resumed in a more normal way.

Identification. The ceremony can cultivate a sense of identity with the deceased. The survivors can be helped to recognize that they have shared the person's life and that they are now, in their own lives, the custodians of the values that he or she lived by. In a sense their lives can be a memorial.

A young man whose career had been joyously and usefully devoted to human service had died. Entering the church for the funeral service, his stricken parents appeared utterly crushed and forlorn.

In the audience were a large number of young people who had known this man and shared his concerns. The speaker talked of the young man's life and what he stood for and went on to say that his ideals and spirit were alive and growing in each of those present. In a very real sense, said the speaker, his effective work was just beginning, and would go forward in the lives of his friends. The response of the listeners could be seen in their faces; most of all, in the faces of the parents. Leaving the church they were almost radiant and one of them remarked, "Wasn't it fine?" Suddenly all these young people had become, in spirit, their children.

Affirmation of Values. It is almost a universal experience that at time of death survivors are prone to think seriously of the meaning of life and to meditate on its values. They are at that time not only open to inspiration but hungry for it. The occasion, therefore, should be used for the enrichment and refinement of life. This is perhaps the most enduring comfort that can be given.

Relief of Guilt.   At a time of death the surviving members of the family are commonly torn between their feelings of love and grief, and the shock and revulsion they tend to feel in the presence of the dead body. It is normal, in this situation, for them to recall their shortcomings with respect to the deceased and to reproach themselves. No human relationship is perfect. A wife recalls how she scolded poor Henry for tracking in the mud. Children remember how they neglected their parents. A husband remembers that Mary never did get that trip to the seashore that she wanted so much. "But it's too late now."

Apparently this is usual. Certainly it is the major basis of many costly and ostentatious funerals. One of the functions of death ceremonies is to gently and quietly remove this sense of guilt through the process of reaffirmation of the values of the deceased. Perhaps the strongest force in lifting the sense of guilt is the reacceptance that the survivors experience from their friends. Love and solidarity help greatly. A thoughtfully planned service provides an excellent opportunity to express this.

Rehabilitation.   When an old person dies after his or her powers have declined greatly from their prime, it is helpful to the survivors to have the memory of this person redirected to the better years of his or her life. Before my father-in-law died, his mental powers had failed and life had become an unhappy burden. His death produced a mixture of grief and thankfulness accompanied by a certain amount of guilt. There was no viewing of the remains. At the memorial service we brought into focus what he was and did in earlier years. From that day we carried with us the image of the fine strong person he had been. No amount of cosmetic restoration could have taken the place of that. In fact, any viewing would have detracted from the desired effect.

Religious Observance.   The occasion of death is an important time to deepen spiritual life, draw on the strength of religious experience and tradition, and unify a congregation. Services planned with the family's clergyman and held in a house of worship can help greatly in this process.

Emotional Support.   A death in the family is like an amputation. The survivors have lost part of themselves and experience intense loneliness and insecurity. The gathering of family, friends and community can be a great source of encouragement and strength. This rallying of support, I might add, should not wait for the funeral or memorial service. Family members and close friends should visit promptly.

A State Funeral.   On the death of a prominent person with whom many people had a meaningful emotional relationship, there is need for a ceremonial in which large numbers of people can take part.

An outstanding case in which these needs were sensitively met was the funeral of President John F. Kennedy. The casket was not opened for public viewing. There were no truckloads of flowers in the funeral procession. Since the entire nation felt a close connection with President Kennedy, an impressive ceremony, widely televised, in which the whole nation could participate, was in good taste and filled an important need.

Three Types of Death Ceremonies

A *funeral service* is, by definition, a service held in the presence of the body, with either an open or closed casket. A *memorial service* is by definition a service held after the body has been removed. It can be either a substitute for a funeral service or in addition to it. A *commitment*, or *committal service* is a brief, optional service held at the graveside or in the chapel of a crematory. It is usually in addition to a funeral or memorial service and is the occasion at which the immediate family and possibly a few close friends bid good-bye to the body.

Ministers and funeral directors are trained in conducting funeral and committal services, but not all have had experience with memorial services. Most of this chapter, therefore, is devoted to memorial services.

Funeral and Committal Services

First, however, I want to offer a few comments on funeral and committal services. These have greater possibilities for variety and for survivor participation than are usually realized. They may be programmed closely or may provide for spontaneous participation.

Many years ago a young priest in Hays, Kansas, read the *Manual* and liked the idea of participation by funeral attenders. He designed a model funeral service which was performed at a national meeting of the Catholic Art Association in which I took part. The service proved to be a skillful blending of Catholic ritual with Quaker sharing of testimony. I recall also an excellent Quaker funeral with a closed casket, at which the funeral director presided and the attenders, including the husband of the woman who had died, did the speaking as they felt moved.

At a funeral, the choice of pallbearers should favor members of the family who may wish to take part. Instead of civic leaders and business associates, the family should have the first chance — including women and teenagers. I have known women who felt deeply deprived because they were excluded from this privilege. The less husky pallbearers should be distributed so that they don't have to lift too much. Indeed, if the box is too heavy, it suggests that the family may have been extravagant in choosing it. Remember also to be careful not to call upon persons with serious heart or back problems. There are more such than we commonly realize.

At a committal service, too, there can be family participation. At my wife's interment I recited one of her favorite poems and helped lower the box into the ground. Family members may be encouraged to start filling in the grave. Such things are emotionally helpful to the survivors.

An important decision to be made in planning a funeral service is the choice between an open or closed casket. It is the overwhelming preference of clergymen—Protestant, Catholic, and Jewish—that the casket be closed. In many cases the viewing of the remains is confined to family members and takes place before the funeral. When family members have been with the body at death or soon after, no later viewing is necessary.

A good "memory image," as funeral directors call it, may be created without viewing the body. Personal reminiscences of the living person can usually generate a better image than viewing the "restored" body.

There are, however, times when cosmetic restoration can be helpful, as when relatives from far away wish to see the body. This does not necessarily require a public viewing. Sensitivity to the wishes of the family should be the key to decisions in this matter.

If a service is held with the casket present, it may be covered with a gray cloth (or pall) as is done, for instance, in Episcopal churches. Thus a solid bronze casket carries no more prestige than a plywood box. This symbolizes the belief that we are all equal in death and helps focus on the spiritual significance of the occasion.

Memorial Services

A memorial service performs much the same function as a funeral service, but tends to have a more positive atmosphere. This is mainly because it is focused on the values of the person who has died instead of on the dead body.

Members of the family should be encouraged—but never pressured—to speak or to offer songs or prayers as they may choose. The following experience is an example of how helpful a memorial service can be, with appropriate family participation.

A friend of mine lost a grown daughter in an automobile accident. He loved her dearly, but there had been some stress between them, and this made her death doubly hard for him. I went to see him and his wife. It happened that I, too, had lost a daughter some time before in a similar accident.

The family were not members of the Society of Friends, but I offered to arrange a memorial service in the Friends Meeting House and suggested that the father might like to speak at such a meeting. They accepted the offer, but he wasn't sure he would be able to speak. However, he called me shortly afterward and said he did indeed want to speak and wanted me to preside.

At the service, the meeting room was decorated with wildflowers and on the mantle was a painting done by the young woman. Her former music teacher played a piece she had especially liked. Then I spoke, saying that we had gathered in the girl's memory and that any who felt moved to speak should feel free to do so. Then the father got up. In his hand was a bunch of little cards, each with a reminder of some incident from his daughter's life, starting from early childhood. He spoke with difficulty at first, but soon became more fluent. As he continued to relate happy memories, a faraway look came into his eyes and he began to smile, and the assembled friends smiled with him.

His wife thought he was speaking too long and tried to catch his eye, but their son, seated next to her, said "Let him talk." And he did, for quite a while. When he sat down there was a period of silence, then their friends spoke in turn, spontaneously, words of comfort and philosophy and reminiscence. When the speaking ran its course and the service was over, it was dark outside. We carried a few chairs into the yard and set candles on them. Friends moved freely inside and outside, visiting with the family and each other. That meeting was, as any good funeral or memorial service should be, the point at which the family could begin to resume normal life and look to the future. They expressed the warmest appreciation.

There was an interesting sequel when a few weeks later the father had occasion to attend the funeral of a business colleague. It was a strictly conventional service at which the minister delivered a cut-and-dried oration—and that was it. My friend was struck by the contrast between the services and was angry at the impersonal and empty character of his friend's funeral.

Self-Planned Services

Some people like to plan their own services. These may be regular funeral services for which the person has selected the readings and music and perhaps the persons to do the readings. Some have planned that their family and friends shall simply come together for a social evening in their memory, with refreshments and fellowship, and perhaps entertainment arranged by the one who has died. Some people make recordings of readings or music to be played at their funeral or memorial services.

Multiple Services

It is often desirable to hold more than one gathering in cases where different groups or distant places are involved. On the occasion of my wife's death, one gathering was held in North Carolina and another in Ohio, and I spoke at both.

Sometimes friends or colleagues in a remote place hold a memorial service independently. This should be fully reported to the family, who will take comfort from it.

No Service at All

Is it ever appropriate to have no funeral or memorial service at all? Yes, under some circumstances this is entirely appropriate. For instance, if the person wanted it that way, the family may properly comply with that wish.

Recently, a young man was killed in an accident two thousand miles from his parents' home. It had been years since he lived with his parents. His work kept him moving from place to place and he had lost contact with his boyhood friends. His parents quite properly decided not to hold a formal service. Friends of the family called at their home to express their love and sympathy.

While death ceremonies do in most cases meet an important need, the decision not to hold a service in a particular situation may be entirely appropriate.

Combination Programs

A mixture of progamming and spontaneous contributions is often a good arrangement. Commonly the program starts with music while people are gathering. If family members or friends are musicians, it is appropriate for them to play. Personal participation is more important than the technical excellence of recorded music. The latter can be used if no musicians are available.

After the opening music an appropriate reading is in order, either poetry or prose. Best of all is some bit of inspirational writing by the person who has died, if this is available. A few suitable selections are offered in Appendix 7, "Sample Death Ceremonies."

Following the reading a brief talk may be given relating to the person who has died. This can be followed by more music and another reading. Attenders can then be invited to share their thoughts, feelings and memories. When this seems to have run its course, there can be more music followed, if desired, by a prayer and/or a period of silence. Attenders should be invited to remain afterwards to visit.

Ceremonies on the Death of the Very Young

The tragic death of a young child presents special problems because of the greater guilt and anger often mingled with the family's grief. If the memorial service is handled wisely the love the parents had for the child often can be channeled into greater affection for one another and for their surviving children. A minister conducting a service can develop this concept, or an attender, if the meeting allows for participation.

The death ceremony for a baby will naturally be less extensive than for an adult or older child, though it should provide an opportunity for friends to give emotional support. It is important to have a ceremony, if only a modest one.

In the case of a stillborn infant, it is well for the family to have a simple ceremony of their own, giving the child a name, recognizing it as a member of the family and honoring its birth and death. Miscarriages and abortions also involve grief, and an informal ceremony can be very helpful. See Chapter 3, "Bereavement," for additional suggestions.

How to Plan a Service

Ideally the family should sit down together, along with their clergyman if they have one, and talk it over. Ann Baty describes this well: "You reminisce, you recall things he said, things he wrote, his ideals, his goals, his plans, his affections—even the annoying things he did. You look over old snapshots. You talk about him and you think about him. From these reflections you begin to plan your ceremony of remembrance." This is a wholesome process that can do much to begin emotional healing.

Time.   The time usually preferred for a memorial service is the same as for a funeral service—two or three days after the death. Evenings and weekends are preferable so that more people can attend. The timing may be modified to meet individual situations, as, for instance, if some member of the family is in the hospital or too far away to come until later. Additional ceremonies at a later date may be appropriate. After my father's death there were two memorial gatherings, followed seven months later by a two day convocation in his memory attended by family and colleagues from far and wide.

Place.   The place of meeting, too, depends on circumstances and should accommodate the expected attendance. To assemble a handful of people in a large hall or sanctuary is forlorn. To turn people away for lack of space is even worse. A familiar place is good. It may be a church or a living room—or even outdoors.

The Format of a Memorial Service

Here are a few basic components with which a memorial service may be planned and procedures to be considered. A service may be designed to use these components in any way the family prefers. Most religious groups have specific worship ceremonies for death, and a clergyman of that faith can assist in preparing and carrying out the plans.

Forms and liturgies may be adapted to include many of the following elements and will in turn suggest other forms and content. Most forms of ritual permit greater flexibility than is generally used. Don't be afraid to express your wishes and explore possibilities.

Instrumental Music.   While people are gathering, it is often good to have some muted organ music, if in a church, or quiet recorded music elsewhere. Or the attenders can gather in silence and have the service begin with music. Music by family and friends is best of all.

I recall a memorial service in my own family, held in a yard beneath the trees, in which by prearrangement the sound of musical chimes from a nearby church (of a different denomination) came through the trees beautifully at just the right time. Music can be interspersed in the program, too, if desired, or used to close it.

Singing.   This is a very desirable form of music for a service, since it allows for participation by family and friends. Unless the song or songs are well known to the attenders, it is good to have song sheets or hymn books available. If printed or duplicated programs are used, words of the songs may be included. Solo or ensemble singing can have a place, especially if done by friends or members of the family. Always encourage family participation.

The Presiding Function.   One individual, generally a minister or a friend of the family, customarily presides, stating the purpose of the gathering and setting the program in motion. This person may or may not also contribute remarks, readings and prayers. If attenders are invited to take part the presiding person will explain when and how this is to be done. The presiding person also signals the end of the service.

Prayers.   For many families, depending on their practice and belief, this is an important part of the service. Prayers may be offered by the minister or other presiding person or by any family member or friend.

Biographical Remarks.   It is often appropriate to give a biographical account of the person's life at the outset of the service. This adds interest and meaning to the service and provides an opportunity for family participation.

Reminiscences.   Whether programmed or unprogrammed, these add greatly to the service and help to convey in depth some feeling of the person's life and values. Family members especially should be encouraged to offer their thoughts and rememberings.

Sometimes certain family members and friends are asked specifically to contribute their recollections, and these are scheduled in sequence to be the main part of the program. I recall a fine memorial service in which a series of speakers had the same topic: "I remember Charlotte."

Don't avoid humorous reminiscences or incidents that may have involved some frustration. If presented in good taste, these carry overtones of affection and a fuller picture of the person's life and personality.

Visual Materials.   The use of films, slides or pictures is sometimes appropriate, if such material is available. A family member, preferably, should do the narrating. A small display of photographs from the life of the person is always appropriate. Sometimes the family likes to have articles present that remind them of the person who has died and that add a touch of intimacy or color. This may take the form of craft or art work, a favorite toy in the case of a child, or something connected with an adult's hobby or profession.

Silence.   Though most commonly associated with Quakers, this practice is observed in many groups, with a period of silence included as part of the service.

Readings.   There is a wealth of beautiful and inspiring poetry, prose and scripture to draw upon. The Bible is a rich source. Likewise the writings of Kahlil Gibran, Rabindranath Tagore and others. These readings can be programmed or, in the case of unprogrammed services, they can be offered by attenders. It is very appropriate to include writings of the person who has died, if available. A few selected readings and sources are listed in Appendix 7, "Sample Death Ceremonies."

Unprogrammed Contributions.   These may constitute the entire service, following the opening music, perhaps a biographical sketch, and introductory remarks in which the attenders are invited to speak. Or they may be called for later in the service, or omitted entirely. It is well for the presiding person to suggest that at least a short period of silence be allowed between speakings.

Care should be taken that time for unprogrammed contributions not be cut short. I have known family members who carried regrets for years that they were cut off from speaking because the service was "running too long."

A word of caution: If the attenders are unfamiliar with the practice of unprogrammed speaking, it may be well to have a few people prepared in advance to begin the speaking.

Visiting After the Service.   It is often desirable for attenders to have an opportunity to visit informally after the service, if facilities allow for this.

Refreshments.   The serving of refreshments during the visiting is a pleasant practice that facilitates conversation. Some may wish to serve a meal after the funeral or memorial service. The custom of the funeral feast is well known. In theory this is supplied by the family of the deceased, but in common practice, it is thoughtful friends and neighbors who supply the food and do the work.

Flexibility

Established procedures are often useful, but they need not be binding. One memorial service was held with everyone seated in a circle. At the close of the service they all stood and joined hands to sing a final song together. Another service (for a golfer) was held as a walking party across a golf course, winding up at the club house for refreshments. Another took the form of a reception at the home of the family whose member had died.

Printed Programs

Programs are not necessary, but sometimes are nice to have. If a service is largely unprogrammed, there is no need for a printed program. If it is highly programmed and especially if it involves group singing, then a program, including the words of songs, can be helpful. This will depend partly on the availability of duplicating equipment. If the service is held in a church, the church may have printed program blanks which can be used. A longer program, perhaps with the full text of the ceremony, also can be used as a death announcement to mail to those who could not attend. This may include a biographical sketch and some personal tributes.

Remember

Grief has many dimensions, which are experienced by different people in different ways. Likewise death ceremonies take many forms. As Ann Baty says, do not be coerced into passive acceptance of a conventional pattern; do not be afraid to be creative. Remember that death is a natural event and an occasion for the honest expression of your deepest values.

8 HOW THE DEAD CAN HELP THE LIVING

This chapter is essentially a tract — an urgent appeal for human solidarity, to persuade people to think in terms of Life and to share with the living any organs or tissues which, at the time of death, they or their loved ones no longer need. To bury or burn organs or tissues needed by the living is a form of blasphemy against life. Let us not be guilty of it. As for myself, I'm leaving my entire body for medical education.

This chapter sets forth the options and the procedures for various types of donations. Directories of medical schools and eye banks, addresses of helpful organizations, and information on transplantation of specific organs will be found in Appendix 8, "Anatomical Gifts."

Poet Robert Test states the issue beautifully:

The day will come when my body will lie upon a white sheet tucked neatly under the four corners of a mattress, located in a hospital busily occupied with the living and the dying. At a certain moment a doctor will determine that my brain has ceased to function and that, for all intents and purposes, my life has stopped.

When that happens, do not attempt to instill artificial life into my body by the use of a machine and don't call this my deathbed. Let it be called the Bed of Life, and let my body be taken from it to help others lead fuller lives.

Give my sight to the man who has never seen a sunrise, a baby's face or love in the eyes of a woman. Give my heart to the person whose own heart has caused nothing but endless days of pain. Give my blood to the teenager who was pulled from the wreckage of his car, so that he may live to see his grandchildren play. Give my kidneys to a person who depends upon a machine to exist from week to week. Take my bones, every muscle, every fiber and nerve in my body and find a way to make a crippled child walk. Explore every corner of my brain. Take my cells, if necessary, and let them grow so that, someday, a speechless boy will shout at the crack of a bat or a deaf girl will hear the sound of rain against her window.

Burn what is left of me and scatter the ashes to the winds to help the flowers grow.

If you must bury something, let it be my faults, my weaknesses and all my prejudice against my fellow man.
Give my sins to the devil. Give my soul to God.

If, by chance, you wish to remember me, do it with a kind deed or word to someone who needs you. If you do all I have asked, I will live forever.[1]

Urgent Need for Anatomical Gifts

In the seventies a historic breakthrough occurred in the transplanting of tissues and organs, starting with the use of cyclosporin. This is a drug which suppresses the immune system without leaving the patient vulnerable to infections as formerly.

In the eighties came the Belzer/UW Organ Preservation Solution, which helps preserve organs and lets them function better and sooner after transplanting.

These developments have resulted in a tremendous increase in transplanting. The American Association of Tissue Banks reports that 450,000 tissue transplants were performed in the United States in 1989, including kidneys, hearts, livers, corneas, pancreas, skin, bone, and lungs.[2] The demand for organs and tissues now exceeds the supply by many thousands. Many potential recipients are not even placed on waiting lists. Daily, people die whose lives might be saved if organs were available. Sight and hearing could be restored to thousands if sufficient corneas and ear structures were donated.

Who May Donate?

Almost everyone is a potential donor. While younger persons are preferred for major organs, persons over sixty may contribute tissues such as corneas, middle ear tissue, bones, skin, and pituitary hormone. For most organs, donations are not accepted from a person who has a contagious or malignant disease or one of unknown cause or who is at high risk of AIDS. Tissues from persons with some disabilities, such as Alzheimer's Disease and ear disorders, are especially needed and requested for research. Post mortem donation of artificial implants with permission to analyze related tissues can also be very helpful for research.

The donation of organs or tissues does not alter the appearance of the dead person at a funeral, nor does it cause him or her the slightest discomfort or inconvenience. The disturbance to the body is generally less than that involved in the routine process of embalming, unless an autopsy is performed as well. There is no cost for organ donation, but the family is still responsible for disposition of the body.

Most religious groups encourage donation. Some Moslem sects, however, do not permit it.

Bequeathal of Entire Body to a Medical School

Thousands of bodies are needed each year for the training of future doctors and dentists. New medical schools are opening, and the supply of unclaimed bodies is diminishing. Only the rapid increase in the practice of bequeathing bodies has averted a nationwide crisis. Bodies may only be given. They may not be sold. Bodies may be donated at death, or after a funeral, with or without viewing, if the funeral director follows the medical school's directions for embalming.

Alternative plans should always be made, through a memorial society if possible, as a medical school's decision to accept a body for study is usually made at time of death, not before. If a bequeathal form has been filed with a medical school in advance, the school may accept the body even though its supplies are ample at the time.

Bequeathal of a body to a medical school, with a memorial service instead of a funeral service, saves the cost of a funeral. However, I recall the case of a man who bequeathed his body to a medical expense, but whose body was autopsied—which made his body unacceptable. As a result he was given a conventional funeral—which bankrupted his family.

Most schools assume responsibility for the final disposition of the body and will, if requested, return the ashes to the family. This may take as long as two years, but generally can be speeded up if desired.

How to Donate Tissues or Organs

There are several ways to donate tissues and organs. For addresses of these organizations, see Appendix 8, "Anatomical Gifts."

1. Discuss your wishes with your family or others who have an emotional stake in this question. Doctors won't remove organs without family approval, even if a donor card has been filled out. Be sure to inform your doctor, close friends, the matron of a nursing home, your executor—anyone who might be involved with handling your body. When admitted to a hospital insist on your wishes being recorded on your patient chart.

2. For donating the entire body, see Appendix 8, "Anatomical Gifts," for instructions on how to make arrangements, together with a directory of medical schools, their degree of need and provision for transportation, or call The Living Bank (800) 528-2971 for information.
3. Carry a Uniform Donor Card signed by yourself and two witnesses. This is legal authority for donation under the Canadian Human Tissue Gift Acts and the U.S. Anatomical Gifts Acts. *Be sure a twenty-four-hour number to call is provided* and carry the card with your driver's license, where it will readily be found in case of accident. See Appendix 8, "Anatomical Gifts," for sources for donor cards.
4. Check the space provided on the driver's license in most states and provinces.
5. Register with the Living Bank (see Appendix 8, "Anatomical Gifts") and carry their donor card with their 24-hour, toll-free number. They have over 285,000 members, as of April, 1990. If called at the time of death, they will immediately contact the nearest appropriate facility to arrange for such anatomical gifts as were desired by the donor. They work with regional and national networks and are especially strategic in rural areas and smaller cities. They receive no tax support. We suggest a contribution if you send for their material.
6. Persons with allergies or other special medical conditions are well advised to register this information with Medic Alert and wear the tag or bracelet they provide. In an emergency they can be called collect for the necessary information, including, if desired, your anatomical gift wishes.
7. For information in Canada, contact Organ Donors Canada, Transplant International, or the transplant coordinator in one of the regional transplant coordinating centers.

Permission for Autopsy

Another service the dead and their families can render is permission for autopsy. Such permission should routinely be granted *except* when the body or a major organ is to be donated. Autopsy is often very helpful in improving the knowledge and experience of doctors and in some cases is more valuable than bequeathal. Sometimes it directly benefits the family. Temporal bones, pituitary and sometimes corneas, skin and bone can be retrieved after an autopsy.

Glasses

Eyeglasses and cases (and brown artificial eyes) left by the dead (or no longer needed by the living) can be sent to New Eyes for the Needy.

They have helped over three million people in the U.S. and other countries since their founding in 1932. In Canada, used eyeglasses are collected and distributed by Operation Eyesight Universal. See Appendix 8, "Anatomical Gifts."

Anatomical Gift Legislation

To encourage anatomical gifts, most American states have, since 1985, adopted laws requiring medical personnel to ask relatives at time of death if organs or tissues may be transplanted to persons in need of them ("required request"). A related measure which is gaining favor in Canada is to require doctors to indicate on the hospital chart that organ donation was considered at the time of death, and if not done, why not. Also in Canada, coroners are increasingly mandated to ask about organ donation in their inquiries following sudden or unexpected deaths. An overwhelming majority of families promptly agree, and it appears a significant increase in donations is resulting.

Going one step beyond this, Finland, Greece, Italy, Norway, Spain and Sweden permit the removal of organs or tissues unless the patient or family expressly objects. Going further still, Austria, Poland, Denmark, Switzerland and France permit such removal regardless of the wishes of the family. In practice, however, doctors won't do it without family permission.

Clearly, these legislative developments will go a long way toward reducing the waste of urgently needed organs and tissues.

Cost of Transplants

Organs for transplant cannot be bought, but the cost of transplantation is often high. Increasingly these costs are being covered by Medicare, Medicaid, Canada's National Health program, and private health insurance companies. Medicaid coverage varies from state to state and from province to province, and private insurance from one company to another. Before buying health insurance, check with the company on this matter.

The Gift of Life

Resolution of the problems of anatomical gifts, and education concerning their desirability will make possible the saving of thousands of lives, cure a vast amount of blindness and relieve much suffering. Consider what it might mean to you. *You* need an organ transplant to save your life. You get one at once. *Your wife* needs a corneal transplant to restore her sight. She gets one immediately. *Your child* needs bone marrow transplants. He receives all he needs. Shortages of organs and tissues could be virtually ended. This gives a wholly new and creative dimension to the human experience of death.

REFERENCES

[1]Used by permission of Robert Test.

[2]American Council on Transplantation.

Many years ago, when we were discussing a man who was being kept alive artificially after any prospect of a useful or satisfying life was past, my mother remarked. "If you let that happen to me, I'll come back and haunt you!"

When, at age 95, she was in a nursing home, bedridden, almost blind and deaf, and unable to speak coherently, my father came to visit her each afternoon, and to give her supper. There was much warmth and tenderness between them, and this continued to give meaning to her life.

At length as her condition deteriorated she decided that she had gone far enough. Her only recourse was to decline food. The nursing home responded with force-feeding—a brutal process. My father protested. "Offer her food," he said. "Give her every consideration, but do *not* force her!" When they ignored his wishes, he brought them a copy of an article Mother had written years before, arguing that a person should be free to end his or her life when his or her physical condition becomes hopeless.[1] Still they persisted, so my father and brother and I jointly called the doctor, saying, "Get the feeding stopped or get her out of there!" This time they stopped and a few days later Mother died in peace.

I took the death certificate to the county health office while my brother fetched a box from the Friends Burial Committee. When we arrived to claim the body the woman in charge exclaimed she had never heard of such a thing. She had called a funeral director who arrived the same time we did. The funeral director graciously turned to the woman in charge and said, "They know what they're doing," then bowed himself out.

We lifted Mother's body into the box and I took it home in my station wagon. In the morning my daughter-in-law and I took her body to the medical school as she had requested. Mother had been firm about this. She was a biologist and thrifty, too. She had said she "didn't want her body wasted." The medical school would have paid for transportation but this was something I could do for her, a meaningful privilege. At the medical school we lifted Mother's body out of the box which we took back for future use.

That afternoon my niece was being married in a nearby city. We all went. The ceremony was of a Quaker type in which there is no presiding minister, the speaking being done by the principals and others who felt moved to speak. This ceremony became a joint celebration of my

89

mother's life and her granddaughter's marriage and was a deeply moving occasion. My father spoke of the "almost unbearable joy" which he felt in the sense of continuity. The next evening we held a Memorial Meeting in the community where Mother had spent most of her life. Family and friends shared their thoughts and memories and extended fellowship and support to one another. That, too, was a memorable occasion which helped to deepen the quality of our lives.

After a few months Mother's ashes were returned, in care of Vicki, my daughter-in-law, who was chairperson of the Burial Committee of the Friends Meeting. Shortly after, our family gathered to bury those ashes at the base of the eighty-ton boulder at Antioch which was designated as a monument to Arthur and Lucy.

A few weeks later there was another development. Vicki received from the medical school another canister of ashes, also purporting to be Lucy's ashes. "What'll we do?" asks Vicki. After some reflection I said, "Just put them in the closet." This was done, and we mentioned it to no one.

Years passed and finally Arthur Morgan, too, died at age ninety-seven. Like Lucy, he left his body to the medical school, and as with Lucy's body, I elected to take it to the medical school myself, with Vicki's help. A series of memorial gatherings were held in Yellow Springs but the main event was a two-day convocation which was held in his memory seven months later, when his ashes would be returned from the medical school. In due time the convocation was held, and people came from far and wide to celebrate his life in a series of events.

One of these events was a ceremony in which his ashes were interred at the base of the boulder. This event was presided over by Donald Harrington, of the Community Church of New York, who had been a student at Antioch during the Morgan era.

In preparation for this event I had taken the canister of Arthur's ashes and the canister with Lucy's "duplicate" ashes and had sealed them together in a small carton. At the appropriate moment this carton was placed in a hole at the base of the boulder by two of Arthur's great grandchildren. No one but Lee and Vicki and I knew that there were two sets of ashes in that carton. As the hole was being filled, Lee remarked to me that it was the only way he could think of "to get Granther to sleep with another woman." How true!

In a more serious vein I reflected that Lucy and Arthur were deeply concerned for humanity and that for an Unknown Human (like the Unknown Soldier!) to share their last resting place seemed eminently fitting.

REFERENCE

[1]"On Drinking the Hemlock," by Lucy G. Morgan. Written in 1927, it was printed in the Dec. 1971 issue of *The Hastings Center Report.*

APPENDIX 1 / *Bibliography*

Resources are listed alphabetically by these sections: General, Living with Dying, Bereavement, Right to Die, and Simple Burial.

General: Books, Pamphlets and Periodicals

Charmaz, Kathy, *The Social Reality of Death: Death in Contemporary America.* Reading, MA: Addison-Wesley Publishing Co., 1980. A clear and comprehensive college textbook covering varied approaches to death, dying, ethics, death in medical settings, "extraordinary death," suicide, the funeral industry, and grief and mourning. Highly recommended.

Compassion Book Service, 216 Via Monte, Walnut Creek, CA 94598. (415) 933-0830. Offers free catalog of books "on Death & Dying, Comfort and Hope." From many different publishers.

Conover, Charlotte Reeve, *Harvest of the Years.* Burnsville, NC: Celo Press, 1931. This classic on aging is a collection of essays by a woman in her eighties. Written with courage and wisdom, it describes the limitations of age with a touch of humor and points the way to rise above them.

Death Studies, Hemisphere Publishing Corporation, 79 Madison Ave., New York, NY 10016, (212) 1725-1999. Quarterly journal of scholarly articles on all aspects of death and dying.

Egendorf, Arthur, *Healing from the War: Trauma and Transformation after Viet Nam.* Houghton Mifflin, 1985. Grieving the many losses we experienced as a nation and as individuals can teach us how to become peacemakers in our daily lives.

Feifel, Herman, *New Meanings of Death.* New York: McGraw Hill, 1977. Outstanding anthology, including articles by Kastenbaum, Bluebond-Langner, Schneidman, Weisman, Garfield, Saunders, Kelly, Kalish, Leviton, Lifton, Simpson, Gutman, and Shaffer and Rodes.

Foos-Graber, Anya, *Deathing.* Nicolas-Hays, Inc., P.O. Box 612, York Beach, ME. A positive approach to death.

Grollman, Earl A. (ed.), *Concerning Death: A Practical Guide for the Living.* Boston: Beacon Press, 1974. Chapters on Protestant, Catholic, and Jewish theology and rituals of death and after life; children and death; final arrangements; bereavement; suicide; and condolence calls and letters.

Hastings Center Report, The Hastings Center, 255 Elm Road, Briarcliff Manor, NY 10510. Bimonthly journal on ethical issues in medicine and life sciences, including death and dying.

Haworth Press, Inc., 10 Alice Street., Binghamton, NY 13904-1580. 1-(800) 3-HAWORTH. Publish four journals and many books relating to death, bereavement, AIDS, cancer and related topics. Send for free catalog.

Head, Joseph and S.L. Cranson (eds.), *Reincarnation: The Phoenix Fire Mystery.* New York: Julian Press/Crown Publishers, Inc., 1977; Warner Books, paper. Comprehensive discussion of major viewpoints about reincarnation.

Irish, Donald P., *Awareness of Death: Preparation for Living.* Religious Education Committee, Friends General Conference, 1502B Race St., Philadelphia, PA 19102, 1976.

Kubler-Ross, Elisabeth, *Death: The Final Stage of Growth.* Englewood Cliffs, NJ: Prentice-Hall, Inc., 1975. Essays on the philosophies of death and after life of Hinduism and Buddhism, practices of Judaism and Alaskan Indians; attitudes of hospital personnel and personal experiences of death as a growthful experience from the perspective of both the dying and the bereaved.

Kubler-Ross, Elisabeth, *On Death and Dying: What the Dying Have to Teach Doctors, Nurses, Clergy and Their Own Families.* New York: Macmillan Publishing Co., 1969. Classic in which the "five stages" of dying are described, based on counseling dying hospital patients. Stresses the need of the dying to be treated as fully alive and human.

Levine, Stephen, *Who Dies? An Investigation of Conscious Living and Conscious Dying.* Garden City, NY: Anchor Press/Doubleday, 1982. Beautiful and practical guide to using the progressive losses of aging and dying as an opportunity for spiritual awakening and a fuller life; applied also to the death of self through which a greater life is gained. Discusses healing, death at home, grief, pain, suicide, funerals, and working with the dying. Universal wisdom from a Zen Buddhist perspective.

Lifton, Robert Jay, M.D., *The Broken Connection.* New York: Simon and Schuster, 1979. Critique of Freudian theories relating to death and immortality with analysis of the effects of the awareness of death. Includes the survivor experience and the pursuit of immortality, analysis of the impact of modern holocaust experiences, and the rise of "nuclearism."

Macy, Joanna, *Despair and Personal Power in the Nuclear Age.* Philadelphia, New Society Publishers, 1983. Confronting our fears of a nuclear holocaust, Macy urges us to feel our pain and transform our numbness into action to promote peace.

Ring, Kenneth, Ph.D., *Life at Death: A Scientific Investigation of the Near Death Experience.* New York: Quill, 1982. Statistical and descriptive studies and interviews about near death experiences from many causes and of many types of people. Explores possible explanations and meanings.

Schneidman, Edwin S., *Death: Current Perspectives.* Palo Alto, CA: Mayfield Publishing Co., 1980. Concepts of death, death as a social disease; demography of death; determination of death; participants of death; survivors of death; life after death; self-destruction; bibliography. Highly recommended.

Living with Dying (See also General listings)

Callari, Elizabeth S., *A Gentle Death*. Tudor Publishers, 3712 Old Battleground Road, Greensboro, NC 27410, 1986.

Duda, Deborah, *Coming Home*. Aurora Press, 388 Calle Colina, Santa Fe, NM 87501, 1982. Practical and comprehensive handbook on financial, physical, emotional, and spiritual aspects of home care through serious illness and death. Highly recommended.

Jury, Mark and Dan, *Gramp*. New York: Grossman Publishers (Viking Press), 1976, paper. A moving and honest account of the death at home of an 82-year-old senile man, reported in word and photograph by his family, who honored his wishes and cared for him with love.

Kelly, Orville E., *Until Tomorrow Comes*. New York: Everest House, 1979. Canada: Beaverbooks. Final book by the founder of the Make Today Count organization, with information about cancer, patient and family reactions, and how to live with cancer. Good for patients, families and caregivers.

Lang, Jennifer M., Judith Spiegel, and Stephen M. Strigle (eds.), *Living With AIDS: A Self-Care Manual*. AIDS Project Los Angeles, 3670 Wilshire Blvd., Suite 300, Los Angeles, CA 90010, 1984. One to nineteen copies, $5.00 plus $.75 mailing, each. Clear descriptions of medical aspects of AIDS and Aids Related Complex; practical instructions for caregivers and self-care at home; psychological and sexual aspects; financial, legal, and insurance matters; national resource directory. Excellent.

LeShan, Eda, *When A Parent Is Very Sick*. Boston: Little Brown & Co., 1986.

Lund, Dores, *Eric*. New York: Dell Publishing Co., 1974. Story of Eric's struggle against leukemia as a young college man, told by his mother.

Mace, Nancy L., and Peter V. Rabins, *The 36-Hour Day: A Family Guide to Caring for Persons with Alzheimer's Disease, Related Dementing Illnesses, and Memory Loss in Later Life*. Baltimore and London: The Johns Hopkins University Press, 1981. Covers medical symptoms and care, problems in independent living, daily care, problems of mood and behavior, effects on caregivers, financial and legal issues, and institutional care. Thorough, readable, practical. An excellent guide.

Martelli, L.J. with F. Peltz and W. Messina, *When Someone You Know Has AIDS*. New York: Crown Publishers, Inc., 1987.

Martinson, I.M., *Home Care for the Dying Child*. New York: Appleton-Century/Croft, 1976.

Upson, Norma S., *When Someone You Love Is Dying*. New York: Simon & Schuster, 1986.

Bereavement (See also General listings)

Arnold, Joan Hagan and Penelope Buschman Gemma, *A Child Dies: A Portrait of Family Grief*. Rockville, MD: Aspen Systems Corporation, 1983. Sensitive discussions of the meaning a child's death has for parents, the process of mourning, and how these vary with the age of the child who dies.

Bereavement Magazine, 350 Gradle Drive, Carmel, IN 46032. Published nine times a year, this magazine is "a warm and caring friend which arrives in your mailbox." A helpful resource. included with each issue is a substantial directory of support groups. An even more substantial directory may be had on request. Send a self-address stamped envelope — business size.) Subscription, $22 per year, $39, two years.

Bozarth-Campbell, Alla, Ph.D., *Life is Good-bye, Life is Hello: Grieving Well Through All Kinds of Loss.* CompCare Publications, 2415 Annapolis Lane, Minneapolis, MN 55441, (800) 328-3330, in Minnesota (612) 559-4800. Sensitive description of many aspects of grieving/healing for all types of loss, written by a woman who is a poet, Gestalt therapist, and Episcopal priest.

Centering Corporation, *Newborn Death.* P.O. Box 3367, Omaha, NE 68103, (402) 553-1200. One of several moving, helpful and inexpensive pamphlets for families losing a child before or shortly after birth. Practical and sensitive advice, and stories, in clear and simple style, for parents and siblings of infants who die or require intensive care.

Corr, Charles, and McNeil, Joan, *Adolescence and Death.* Springer, 1986. Describes ways adolescents encounter death, dying and bereavement and identifies developmentally appropriate ways to help.

DiGiulio, Robert C., *Beyond Widowhood.* The Free Press (A division of Macmillan), 866 Third Ave., New York, NY 10022. Combines the training of a scholarly teacher with the experience of widowhood.

Grollman, Earl A., *Talking About Death: A Dialogue Between Parent and Child.* Boston: Beacon Press, 1971. Models a direct and gentle way of discussing a death in the family, exploring the child's feelings and reassuring him or her.

Hewett, John H., *After Suicide.* Philadelphia: Westminster, 1980.

Jensen, Amy Hillyard, *Healing Grief.* Medic Publishing Co., P.O. Box 89, Redmond, WA 98073, (206) 881-2883, 1980. An inexpensive pamphlet with concise, comprehensive and helpful information for bereaved parents. Highly recommended.

Kohn, William K. and Jane Burgess Kohn, *Widower.* Boston: Beacon Press, 1978. A widower relates his personal experiences, including comment based on interviews with many other widowers.

Krementz, Jill, *How It Feels When a Parent Dies.* New York: Alfred A. Knopf, 1983.

LeShan, Eda, *Learning to Say Good-bye.* New York: Macmillan, 1976. Also Avon paperback. A loving, sensitive book for children ages 9–10.

Levine, Stephen, *Healing into Life and Death.* New York: Anchor Press/Doubleday, 1987. Might be considered a refinement of *Who Dies?,* with profound commentary and guided meditations of healing grief and dis-ease.

Moffat, Mary Jane, *In the Midst of Winter: Selections from the Literature of Mourning.* New York: Vintage Books, 1982.

Neeld, Elizabeth Harper, *Seven Choices.* Clarkson Potter, Inc., 1990. The writer's sensitive narrative of life after the death of her young husband, followed by accounts of other individuals and how they found new equilibrium after loss. Comprehensive analysis and advice.

O'Toole, Donna, *Aarvy Aardvark Finds Hope.* Rainbow Connection, 477 Hannah Branch Road, Burnsville, NC 28714, 1988. A charming read-aloud story for all ages, about living and losing, friendship and hope.

O'Toole, Donna, *Bridging the Bereavement Gap: A Manual for the Preparation and Programming of Hospice Bereavement Services,* 1985. Rainbow Connection, Burnsville, NC 28714.

O'Toole, Donna, *Growing Through Grief: A K–12 Curriculum to Help Young People Through All Kinds of Loss.* Rainbow Connection (address above). Award-winning curriculum written in three age group sections. Extensive background material, annotated resources and activity sheets for reproduction. 382 pages — a major resource.

O'Toole, Donna, *Healing and Growing Through Grief.* Published by Blue Cross and Blue Shield of Michigan, 1986; available from the Rainbow Connection, Burnsville, NC 28714. Simple, clear, practical explanation of grief reactions and how to find your way through them to fuller life. Highly recommended.

Panuthos, Claudia, and Catherine Romeo, *Ended Beginnings: Healing Childbearing Losses,* South Hadley, MA: Bergin & Garvey, 1984. Discusses infant deaths from Sudden Infant Death Syndrome, stillbirth, miscarriage, and abortion, as well as infertility, C-section and difficult births. Explores physical emotional and spiritual aspects; includes many personal stories.

Rando, Theresa A., *Grief, Dying and Natural Death: Clinical Interventions for Caregivers.* Champaign, IL: Research Press Company, 1984. A practical, no nonsense approach with a good overview of theory and intervention strategies for working with the dying, the bereaved, children and ourselves.

Rando, Theresa A., *Grieving: How to Go on Living When Someone You Love Dies.* Lexington, MA: D.C. Heath and Co., 1988.

Riemer, Jack, *Jewish Reflections on Death.* New York: Schocken Books, 1974. An anthology reflecting the psychological and spiritual wisdom of Jewish law and tradition concerning death and mourning. Explores modern problems relating to death, from the Jewish experience of suffering and solace.

Sanford, Doris, *It Must Hurt a Lot: A Book about Death and Learning and Growing.* Portland, OR: Multinomah Press, 1985.

Schatz, William H., *Healing a Father's Grief.* 1984. Medic Publishing Co., P.O. Box 89, Redmond, WA, (206) 881-2883. For bereaved fathers; direct and practical; highly recommended.

Stearns, Ann Kaiser, *Living through Personal Crisis.* New York: Ballantine Books, 1984.

Sullender, R. Scott, *Grief and Growth: pastoral Resources for Emotional and Spiritual Growth.* Paulist Press. Written for Christian clergy but has broader appeal. Explains the role meaning plays in bereavement and personal growth for grieving people. Explains effective use of ritual during grief.

Tatelbaum, Judy, *The Courage to Grieve.* New York: Lippincott & Crowell, 1980.

Viniga, Robert, *A Gift of Hope: How We Survive our Tragedies.* Boston: Little, Brown and Company, 1985. Very readable and moving guide to process of grief and transformation through large and small losses.

Warden, J. William, *Grief Counselling and Grief Therapy: A Handbook for the Mental Health Practitioner*. New York: Springs Publishing Co., 1982. This short work outlines both the stages of grieving, the tasks associated with each stage and the consequent appropriate interventions. A classic resource for practitioners.

Watson, Elizabeth, *Guests of My Life*. Burnsville, NC: Celo Press, 1979. Moving personal account of a mother's journey through grief for the loss of her grown daughter. Describes the insight and comfort received from works of Tagore, Whitman, Dickinson, Mansfield, Paton and Rilke.

Westberg, Granger F., *Good Grief: A Constructive Approach to the Problem of Loss*. Philadelphia: Fortress Press, 1962 and 1971. Available in regular or large print. For the layman, brief and clear descriptions of the phases of grief, for all faiths.

Wolfert, Alan, *Helping Children Cope with Grief*. Muncie, IN: Accelerated Development, Inc., 1983. A practical and helpful book for parents, teachers and counsellors.

Wolterstorff, Nicholas, *Lament for a Son*. Grand Rapids, MI: William B. Eerdmans Publishing Co., 1987. Brief, very honest and moving personal account of a father's grief. Christian perspective on the mysteries of suffering and death, with no easy answers.

Wylie, Betty Jane, *The Survival Guide for Widows*. New York: Ballantine Books, 1982.

Right to Die

Alvarez, A., *The Savage God*. New York: Random, 1972. Historical, literary and philosophical review of suicide, including descriptions of Alvarez's friendship with Sylvia Plath and his own suicide attempt.

Brodie, Howard, *Ethical Decisions in Medicine*. Boston: Little, Brown & Co., 1976. Examines issues of informed consent, quality of life, ethical participation, allocation of scarce resources, and euthanasia. Highly recommended.

The Euthanasia Review, quarterly. Human Sciences Press, Inc., 72 Fifth Ave., New York, NY 10011-8004, (212) 243-6000.

Giovaccini, Peter, *The Urge to Die: Why Young People Commit Suicide*. New York: Penguin, 1983.

Humphry, Derek, *Let Me Die before I Wake: Hemlock's Book of Self-Deliverance for the Dying*. The Hemlock Society, P.O. Box 66218, Los Angeles, CA 90066, 1981. Case stories of assisted suicides by terminally ill persons; compassionate discussion of emotional, legal and physical aspects of self-deliverance.

Klagsbrun, Francine, *Too Young to Die: Youth and Suicide*. New York: Pocket Books, 1981. Most youthful suicides could be prevented by learning the danger signals and knowing what to do. Highly recommended.

Law Reform Commission of Canada, *Euthanasia, Aiding Suicide and Cessation of Treatment*, 1982. Available by mail, free, from the Commission at 130 Albert St., 7th Floor, Ottawa, K1A 0L6. Canada. Clear and comprehensive discussion.

Maguire, Daniel C., *Death by Choice*. New York: Schocken Books, 1974, paper. Marquette University theologian wrestles with ethical questions of death by choice: deciding for yourself, deciding for others; legal killing (abortion, capital punishment, war). Highly recommended.

Simple Burial (See also Appendix 6—CAFMS Publications.)

Bowman, LeRoy, *The American Funeral*. Westport, CT: Greenwood Press, reprinted 1973. Classic sociological study.

Carlson, Lisa, *Caring for Your Own Dead*, Hinesburg, VT: Upper Access Publishers, 1987. Detailed information on cremation and home burial and on the laws, procedures and crematories in each state. Highly recommended for those considering burying their own dead without the assistance of a memorial society.

Consumers Union, *Funerals: Consumers' Last Rights*. Mount Vernon: NY 10550, 1977. Detailed and comprehensive discussion of consumer options in funeral arrangements, including relevant laws, autopsy, and costs.

Continental Association, *Bulletin*, 2001 S Street, NW, Washington DC 20009. Monthly publication of the Continental Association of Funeral and Memorial Societies, consumer viewpoint on events and trends in the funeral industry and memorial society movement.

Dacey, Norman F., *How To Avoid Probate—Updated*. New York: Crown Publishers, Inc., revised, 1987. Has helped many families reduce legal costs following death. Explains the process of probate and provides forms for filing an "inter vivos" trust. Helpful only if used before death.

Mitford, Jessica, *The American Way of Death*. New York: Fawcett, 1979, paper. Witty expose of funeral industry practices which created a national sensation. Out of print, but still highly relevant; check your library for a copy.

APPENDIX 2 / Organizations

(For organizations related to donation of tissues, organs and bodies, see Appendix 8. For a more comprehensive directory of support groups consult *Bereavement Magazine*, listed in Appendix 1, "Bibliography.")

Alzheimer's Disease and Related Disorders Association, Inc., 70 E. Lake St., Suite 600, Chicago, IL 60601, (312) 853-3060. 210 chapters, 1,600 support groups. Research, education, support, public policy, family services. Newsletter and literature.

American Association of Suicidology, Dept. of Health, 2459 S. Ash, Denver, CO 80222, (303) 692-0985. Educational programs and publications to advance the study of suicide prevention and life threatening behavior.

American Cancer Society, 1599 Clifton Rd., NE, Atlanta, GA 30329. 58 divisions and over 3000 local groups sponsors self-help support groups and other services for cancer patients and their families. National programs of research and education.

Americans Against Human Suffering, 2505 Canada Blvd., Glendale, CA 91206. The political wing of the Hemlock Society, working to pass the Humane and Dignified Death Act, giving terminally ill patients the right to request a physician to aid their dying through an overdose of drugs.

Association for Death Education and Counseling, 638 Prospect Ave., Hartford, CT 06105, (203) 567-0329. For death education teachers and counselors in U.S. and Canada. $50 annual membership includes newsletter, discounts on *Death Studies* and *Canadian Journal on Aging.*

The Candlelighters Childhood Cancer Foundation, 1312 18th Street NW, Suite 200, Washington DC 20036, (202) 659-5136, and 1-(800) 366-2223. An international organization of 250 self-help groups of parents of children/ adolescents with cancer. Quarterly and Youth Newsletter. Bibliography.

Cemetery Consumer Service Council, P.O. Box 3574, Washington, DC 20007, (703) 379-6426. Industry-sponsored agency to respond to consumer complaints. Assists state cemetery boards and trade associations to establish guidelines and standards; forwards and, if necessary, mediates consumer complaints.

Centering Corporation, P.O. Box 3367, Omaha, NE 68103-0367 (402) 553-1200. Nonprofit, tax exempt, provides workshops, newsletter, filmstrips and booklets for children and for siblings and parents bereaved through miscarriage, newborn death, death of older children or grandparents. Highly recommended.

The Compassionate Friends, P.O. Box 3696. (708) 990-0010. A national self-help organization for bereaved parents. Has material also for bereaved siblings. 620 chapters. Annual conference.

Continental Association of Funeral and Memorial Societies See Appendix 6, "Directory of Memorial Societies."

Cremation Association of North America, 401 N. Michigan Ave., Chicago, IL 60601, (312) 644-6610. Industry trade association. Offers brochures on cremation and memorialization.

Elisabeth Kubler-Ross Center, South Route 616, Head Waters, VA 24442. Healing and growth center founded by Elisabeth Kubler-Ross; educational and inspirational materials, newsletter, counseling, and workshops.

Foundation for Hospice and Home Care, 519 C Street, N.E., Stanton Park, Washington, DC 20002, (202) 547-6586. Research and educational materials and programs for advancement of care for the disadvantaged, disabled, debilitated and aged, through alternatives to institutional care.

Foundation of Thanatology, 630 W. 168th St., New York, NY 10032, (212) 928-2066. Quarterly newsletter. Extensive library, symposia on psychological aspects of death and dying. Scientific and theoretical emphasis. Offer book catalog.

Funeral Service Consumer Assistance Program, carried on by the National Research and Information Center, 1600-1628 Central St., Evanston, IL 60201, 1-(800) 662-7666. This agency succeeded THANACAP, which was a program of the National Funeral directors Association. Unlike THANACAP it is run by a nonprofit organization. They report about one complaint per week (from 37,000 funerals).

Grief Education Institute, 1780 S. Bellaire St., Suite 132, Denver, CO 80220, (303) 758-6048. Offers support groups for bereaved and education programs on grief resolution. Training manual available; Bereavement Support Groups; Leadership Manual. Prepaid, $25.

Grief Resource Foundation, P.O. Box 28551, Dallas, TX 75228, (214) 279-8900. Provides grief and death education, training, information and referral to health care providers, social workers, clergy and others. Broad assortment of reading materials.

The Hastings Center, 255 Elm Rd., Briarcliff Manor, NY 10510, (914) 782-8500. Publishes bimonthly *Hastings Center Report,* articles, book reviews, and annual annotated bibliographies, and holds conferences on biomedical ethics.

The Hemlock Society, P.O. Box 11830, Eugene, OR 97440, (503) 342-5740. Provides information and support for voluntary euthanasia (self-deliverance) for terminally ill adults and also for the seriously, incurably physically ill. Member of the World Federation of Right-to-Die Societies.

Hospice of Marin, 150 Nellen Ave., Core Madera, CA 94925 (415) 927-2273. Local hospice with strong national outreach for information and training.

International Association for Widowed People, P.O. Box 3564, Springfield, IL 62708. Offers services to widowed people and support groups in developing programs and activities for widowed people. Quarterly newsletter, and *Survivors International* Magazine. Also seminars and conferences for widowed people.

Loving Outreach for Survivors of Sudden-Death (L.O.S.S.), P.O. Box 7303, Stn. M, Edmonton, Alberta T5E 6C8, Canada, (403) 476-7035. Outreach to survivors, whether death of loved one recent or some time ago. Send $2 for packet of information helpful to bereaved. Please note relationship to deceased and how and when death occurred.

Minnesota Coalition for Death Education and Support, P.O. Box 6799, St. Paul, MN 55106, (612) 779-4397. Bibliographies, speakers, information on local resources, educational programs. Newsletter, $15 a year.

Monument Builders of North America, 1612 Central St., Evanston, IL 60201. (708) 869-2031. Process complaints on burial monuments.

National AIDS Hotline, Center for Disease Control, Public Health Service. 1-(800) 342-HELP.

National AIDS Information Clearing House, 1-(800) 458-5231. Will provide literature.

National Association for Widowed People, P.O. Box 3564, Springfield, IL 62708. 23,000 local groups, newsletter & quarterly periodical.

National Coalition for Fair Funeral Prices, P.O. Box 2266, Phoenix, AZ 85002, (602) 838-0297. See pages 51, 114.

National Funeral Directors Association, 11121 W. Oklahoma Ave., Milwaukee, WI 53227, (414) 541-2500. Leading trade association. Provides literature, audiovisual materials and speakers on many aspects of bereavement and funeral planning.

National Hospice Organization. See Appendix 3, "Hospice Organizations."

National Institute on Drug Abuse, Drug Information & Treatment Hotline 9 A.M. to 3 P.M. Mon.–Fri. 12 noon to 3 P.M. Sat.–Sun. EST. 1-(800) 662-HELP.

National Self-Help Clearing House, Graduate School and University Center, City University of New York, 33 West 42nd St., Room 620N, New York, NY 10036, (212) 642-2944. Provides information on peer support groups of all kinds, and how to organize them.

National Sudden Infant Death Syndrome Foundation, 10500 Little Patuxent Parkway, Suite 420, Columbia, MD 21044, 1-(800)-221-SIDS. 68 chapters, national information and referral service, newsletter.

Parents of Murdered Children and other Survivors of Homicide Victims, 100 E. 8th St., Rm. B-41, Cincinnati, OH 45202. Founded by parent survivors in 1978 for parents and other survivors of murder victims. Provides information, advocacy and newsletter to meet the unique needs of murder survivors. Local support groups.

Pregnancy and Infant Loss Center, 1421 E. Wayzata Blvd., Suite 40, Wayzata, MN 55391, (612) 473-9372. Support, referral, and education after miscarriage, stillbirth and newborn death.

Seasons: Suicide Bereavement, P.O. Box 187, Park City, UT 84060. Information and referral for "survivor-victims" of suicide. Local support groups.

SHARE, St. Elizabeth Hospital, 211 S. 3rd St., Belleville, IL 62222. Founding group for infant death support groups.

St. Mary's Grief Support Center, 407 East 3rd St., Duluth, MN 55805-4402. (218) 726-4402. Conducts specialized support groups for children, youth, adults, siblings, parents, infertile couples. Provides literature and useful prototypes.

St. Francis Center, 5417 Sherier Pl., N.W., Washington, DC 20016, (202) 363-8500. Nonsectarian organization providing professional counseling, education, and training, and volunteer support to individuals and organizations facing life-threatening illness and bereavement. Publishes quarterly journal, *Centering* for membership and *Living with AIDS: Perspectives for Caregivers,* a training manual for caregivers. Annual workshop series for health and mental health professionals, school personnel and community on psychosocial issues of illness and grief.

Suicide Prevention Center, Inc., P.O. Box 1393, Dayton, OH 45401-1393. Provides pamphlets, manuals, audiovisuals, including after a suicide death. Business office (513) 223-9096, Crisis line: (513) 223-4777.

Society for the Right to Die, 250 W. 57th St., New York, NY 10107, (212) 246-6973. Distributes many publications including the Living Will, lobbies for Natural Death Act Laws, provides educational materials and programs including information on legislation and court decisions relating to the right-to-die.

Widowed Persons Service, American Association of Retired Persons, 1909 K St., N.W., Washington, DC 20049, (202) 728-4370. Provides assistance in developing local support programs for widowed people, public education about needs of the widowed and services available, directory of services for widowed persons. Free pamphlet "On Being Alone."

APPENDIX 3 / *Hospice Organizations*

National Hospice Organization. 1901 N. Moore St., Suite 901, Arlington, VA 22209, 703-243-5900. NHO is the national coordinating body for hospice organizations. It sponsors national and regional meetings, develops standards of care, provides education materials and newsletter, and advocates for hospice to government and private insurance programs. A directory of the state hospice organizations will be found on the following pages.

Hospice Education Institute. P.O. Box 713, Essex, CT 06426-0713, 800-331-1620; except in Connecticut and Alaska call 203-767-1620. Through their computerized "Hospicelink", HEI refers callers immediately to the nearest hospice. Also coordinates regional, national and international seminars and training for hospice professionals, health care providers, and civic groups; presents community education programs; consultation to existing hospice programs and to groups seeking to begin hospice care.

Financial Help for Terminal Care

Medicare.   This is an insurance program administered by the Social Security System for recipients of Social Security payments. Medicare A covers some home health services provided by a state certified home health agency, if a patient is homebound, in need of skilled nursing service, and under a doctor's plan of treatment. Covered services may include skilled nursing, home health aids, medical equipment and supplies, and medical social work. There is co-payment of twenty percent for equipment and appliances.

Since 1983, Medicare has also provided an optional hospice benefit for eligible patients who are certified as having less than six months to live. A person who signs up for the Hospice Benefit automatically waives Medicare A coverage for the terminal illness while under the care of hospice. Covered services may include physical and occupational therapy, speech therapy, homemaker services, medical supplies, physician's services, short-term inpatient care, respite care for the family, and counseling, including bereavement counseling. Services must be provided by a federally certified hospice, meeting Medicare's standards for scope of services, written plans for patient care, and centralized recordkeeping and administration. Benefits are paid according to a set daily rate, and need not be separately authorized.

Because of the rigorous standards for certification, many smaller hospices have not applied for certification and therefore are not eligible for Medicare payment. There is concern that as hospice becomes an institutionalized part of our health care system, it may tend to lose its former spirit of volunteerism, enthusiasm, and flexibility in meeting the needs of patients, families and communities.

103

Medicaid.   This is a state-supervised, county-administered program whose benefits and requirements vary from state to state. If your income is near the poverty level and you own no more than your house, car and minimal savings, you may be eligible. Your county social services agency can tell you the requirements and determine your eligibility. Medicaid generally has a deductible amount ("spenddown") after which it covers one hundred percent of such expenses as medicines, skilled nursing, doctor's visits, medical supplies, and appliances. This program is especially important for those under sixty-five who do not quality for Medicare.

Private Insurance.   Many insurance policies cover some home health care services, even without specific hospice benefits, and increasingly companies are including a provision for hospice coverage as part of standard benefits or as supplemental coverage offered separately. Counselling and bereavement services are not normally included. Generally there is little or no additional premium. When a hospice program is not certified, a company will make its own assessment to decide about reimbursing the provider agency. Companies are more likely to cover home care if it can be demonstrated that this will enable them to save hospital costs. Inquire of individual companies, preferably in advance of need, to determine the specific benefits they offer.

Other Assistance.   Housekeeper or chore services, home health aides, health appliances, and other support services may be available from other sources. Senior citizen programs, private social service agencies, and private health-related organizations offer a variety of help to those eligible. Hospital, health department, and hospice social workers, and community information-and-referral services can provide leads. It is sometimes surprising what services can be discovered if one is persistent and keeps asking for suggestions.

Tips on Dealing with Bureaucracies.   Always make a note of the date of any conversation, the person you spoke with and the substance of what was said. Keep an orderly file of all written communication. If delays and/or contradictions arise, this will make it much easier to check back on your understanding and resolve the problem. If delay or confusion persists, don't hesitate to ask for a resolution from a supervisor. In most offices there is someone you can talk to as one human being to another. Keep going until you find that person.

Some local and many state governments have telephone numbers which citizens may call to obtain accurate information about government programs. Local employees may be confused by frequent changes in regulations. Also, you can ask a hospital or health department social worker, or a citizen advocacy group.

State Hospice Headquarters or Contacts

This directory was up-to-date as of early 1990, but state headquarters are frequently shifted. Should any of the following be obsolete, you can get the current address and phone number from the responding party or from the National Hospice Organization, listed at the beginning of this Appendix.

ALABAMA: Alabama Hospice Organization, 912 River Haven Circle, Hoover 35244 (205) 733-0166

ALASKA: Hospice of Anchorage, 3605 Arctic Blvd., #555, Anchorage 99503 (907) 561-5322

ARIZONA: Ariz. Hospice Organization, East Valley Hospice, 1450 S. Dobson, Ste. B-322, Mesa 85202 (602) 835-0711

ARKANSAS: Arkansas State Hospice Assn., 1501 N. University, Ste. 400, Little Rock 72207 (501) 664-7870

CALIFORNIA: California State Hospice Organization, P.O. Box 11186, Torrance 90510 (213) 534-5600

COLORADO: Colorado State Hospice Organization, P.O. Box 2270, Evergreen 80439 (303) 674-6400

CONNECTICUT: Hospice Council of Connecticut, 60 Lorraine Street, Hartford 06105 (203) 233-2222

DELAWARE: Delaware Hospice, Inc., 3519 Silverside Rd., Ste. 100, Wilmington 19810 (302) 478-5707

DISTRICT OF COLUMBIA: Hospice Care of the DC, 1749 St. Matthews Ct. NW, Washington 20036 (202) 347-1700

FLORIDA: Fla. Hospices, Inc., Brevard Hospice, Inc., P.O. Box 560965, Rockledge 32956 (407) 636-2211

GEORGIA: Georgia Hospice Organization, Hospice of Athens, 2092 Prince Ave., Athens 30606 (404) 548-8923

HAWAII: Hawaii State Hospice Network, St. Francis Medical Center, 24 Pulwa Road, Honolulu 96817 (808) 537-6011

IDAHO: Idaho Hospice Org., Hospice of North Idaho, 2003 Lincoln Way, Coeur d'Alene 83814 (208) 667-4537

ILLINOIS: Illinois State Hospice Organization, 305 S. Illinois St., Ste. 100, Belleville 62220 (618) 235-7755

INDIANA: Indiana Assoc. of Hospices, St. Vincent Hospice, P.O. Box 80160, Indianapolis 46280 (317) 875-4696

IOWA: Iowa Hospice Org., 8364 Hickman Rd., Ste. D, Des Moines 50322 (515) 253-0875

KANSAS: Kansas State Hospice Org., Phillips County Area Hospice, Box 607, Phillipsburg 67661 (913) 543-5266 x 250

KENTUCKY: Kentucky Assn. of Hospices, Lourdes Hospice, 1530 Lone Oak Rd., Paducah 42002 (502) 444-2262

LOUISIANA: La. Hospice Org., Schumpert Med. Ctr. Hospice, 335 Margaret Place, Shreveport 71120 (318) 227-4605

MAINE: Maine Hospice Council, 11 Parkwood Drive, Augusta 04330 (207) 622-7566

MARYLAND: Hospice Network of Md., 5820 Southwestern Blvd, Ste. 100-A, Baltimore 21227 (301) 242-1975

MASSACHUSETTS: Hospice Care at Southwood Community Hospital, 111 Dedham St., Norfolk 02056 (508) 668-0385 x 288

MICHIGAN: Michigan Hospice Organization, 233 E. Fulton, Ste. 114, Grand Rapids 49503 (616) 454-1426

MINNESOTA: Minn. Hospice Org., Riverside Med. Ctr., 25th and Riverside, Minneapolis 55454 (612) 337-4217

MISSISSIPPI: Gulf Coast Community Hospice, 545 16th St., #36, Gulfport 39507 (601) 896-7483

MISSOURI: Mo. Hospice Org., 9414 Pine Av., St. Louis 63144 (314) 962-9115

MONTANA: Montana Hospice Org., Mtn West HH & Hospice, 500 N. Higgins, Ste. 201, Missoula 59802 (406) 728-8848

NEBRASKA: Nebraska Hospice Organization, H Hlth/Beatrice Comm Hosp, 1201 S 9, Beatrice 68310 (402) 223-2366

NEVADA: Janet Cowley, c/o Nathan Adelson Hospice, 4141 S. Swenson Street, Las Vegas 89119 (702) 733-0320

NEW HAMPSHIRE: Home Health & Hospice Care, 22 Prospect St., Nashua 03060 (603) 882-2941

NEW JERSEY: New Jersey Hospice Organization, 760 Alexander Road, CN 1, Princeton 08540 (609) 275-4125

NEW MEXICO: New Mexico Assn. for Home Care, 1339 Cerrillus Rd., Ste. 6, Santa Fe 87501 (505) 982-9962

NEW YORK: New York State Hospice Association, 468 Rosedale Avenue, White Plains 10605 (914) 946-7699

NORTH CAROLINA: Hospice of North Carolina, 1046 Washington St., Raleigh 27605 (919) 829-9588

NORTH DAKOTA: N.D. Hospice Org., United Hospice, 1133 S. Columbia Rd., Grand Forks 58201 (701) 780-5258

OHIO: Ohio Hospice Organization, 3137 W. Broad St., Columbis 43204 (614) 274-9513

OKLAHOMA: Okla. Hospice Org., Eastern Okla. Hospice, 2012 A West Okmulgee, Muskogee 74401 (918) 683-1192

OREGON: Oregon Hospice Association, P.O. Box 10796, Portland 97210 503-229-7546

PENNSYLVANIA: Pa. Hospice Network, Hospice Care, Inc. P.O. Box 1316, 55 Highland Ave., Washington 15301 (412) 627-8118

PUERTO RICO: Luz M. Gonzalez, Hospicio La Providencia, P.O. Box 10447, Ponce 00732 (809) 843-2364

RHODE ISLAND: Hospice Care of Rhode Island, Potter Building, 345 Blackstone Blvd., Providence 02906 401-272-4900

SOUTH CAROLINA: Hospice of South Carolina, 1807 Marsh Avenue, Florence 29501 803-662-2978

SOUTH DAKOTA: South Dakota Hospice Organization, 172 4th St., SE, Huron 57350 (605) 352-8802

TENNESSEE: Tenn. State Hospice Org., Hospice of Murfreesboro, 310 N. University, Murfreesboro TN 37130 (615) 896-4663

TEXAS: Texas Hospice Organization, 1600 Heather Glen Ct., Richardson 75081 (214) 783-1457

UTAH: Utah Hospice Organization, Hospice of IHC Home Care, 1875 S. State T500, Orem 84058 (801) 225-0584

VERMONT: Hospice Council of Vermont, 52 State Street, Montpelier 05602 802-229-0579

VIRGINIA: VA Assoc. for Hospice, 7814 Carousel Lane, #300, Richmond 23229 804-346-0862

WASHINGTON: Wash. Hospice Org., St. Elizabeth Medical Center, 110 S 9th Ave., Yakima 98902 (509) 575-5163

WEST VIRGINIA: Hospice Council of W.V., Hospice of Huntington, P.O. Box 464, Huntington 25701 (304) 529-4217

WISCONSIN: Wisconsin Hospice Organization, 7 N. Pinckney, Ste. 110, Madison 53703 (608) 257-2611

WYOMING: Wyoming Hospice Organization, Hospice of Sweetwater Cnty, 425 Centennial, Rock Springs 82935 (307) 362-1990

APPENDIX 4 / *Living Will*

A **Living Will** declaration is a document instructing one's doctor and family to refrain from measures to prolong the process of dying when one is terminally ill and unable to communicate one's wishes. In 1986, thirty eight states and the District of Columbia had adopted living will legislation and bills had been introduced in eleven other states: Kentucky, Massachusetts, Michigan, Minnesota, Nebraska, New Jersey, New York, Ohio, Pennsylvania, Rhode Island, and South Dakota. Only North Dakota had taken no action. In 1985, the U.S. National Conference of Commissioners on Uniform State Laws approved a "Uniform Rights of the Terminally Ill Act," recommending it for adoption throughout the U.S.

Detailed information on the Uniform Act and on the individual state laws is available from the Society for the Right To Die, 250 West 57th Street, New York, NY 10107, (212) 246-6973.

Living Will Declaration

Following is the Living Will Declaration which the Society for the Right to Die recommends when no state form is provided:

To My Family, Doctors, and All Those Concerned with My Care

I, _____, being of sound mind, make this statement as a directive to be followed if I become unable to participate in decisions regarding my medical care.

If I should be in an incurable or irreversible mental or physical condition with no reasonable expectation of recovery, I direct my attending physician to withhold or withdraw treatment that merely prolongs my dying. I further direct that treatment be limited to measures to keep me comfortable and to relieve pain.

These directions express my legal right to refuse treatment. Therefore I expect my family, doctors, and everyone concerned with my care to regard themselves as legally and morally bound to act in accord with my wishes, and in so doing to be free of any legal liability for having followed my directions.

I especially do not want:

[enumerate]

Other Instructions/comments:

[list them]

107

Proxy Designation Clause: Should I become unable to communicate my instructions as stated above, I designate the following person to act in my behalf:

[Give name and address]

If the person I have named above is unable to act in my behalf, I authorize the following person to do so:

[Give name and address]

Signed: _____ Date: _____

Witness: _____ Witness: _____

(Keep the signed original with your personal papers at home. Give signed signed copies to doctors, family, and proxy. Review your Declaration from time to time; initial and date it to show it still expresses your intent.)

An Alternative Living Will

This form was drafted and signed by Ernest Morgan and endorsed in writing by his family and physician

I want to have some control over my own death. In the event of *any* illness I want to know whether any given treatment is for recovery or life support, or whether it is for comfort. And I want to be free to accept or decline any specific treatment. In the event of my incapacity to make such decisions, because of unconsciousness or other condition, for more than 24 hours, that circumstance shall constitute a decision against treatment directed toward recovery or life support.

When death does come I want to go as gracefully and comfortably as possible, and not be held back by well-meaning medics and family.

[Add Organ Donor Provision, below, if desired.]

Signed: _____ Date: _____

We accept and support Ernest's perspective in this matter.

[Signed by wife, children and personal physician]

(The above document is appropriate to persons over sixty-five. For younger persons a longer period should be specified.)

(Additional Provision For Organ Donors)

However, I have bequeathed organs of my body for medical purposes. Therefore, if my body is brain dead, I wish and authorize the use of organ/tissue support procedures, but at no expense to my survivors or my estate, to keep those tissues alive until a qualified surgical team can remove them.

Statement to Accompany Donated Organs

I am attaching the following statement, signed only "The Donor and family" to my living will and whatever other documents will give it the best chance of coming into the hands of person(s) receiving organs or tissues from my body.

I am pleased with the prospect that organs or tissues from my body may, after my death, find service in the life of another. This symbolizes, in a tangible way, the unity of life.

To you, the recipient, I offer gratitude for making me a participant in your life and for helping add a creative dimension to my death. May you enjoy health and happiness.

— The Donor and family.

Burial Boxes

Repeatedly people have asked where to buy, or how to build, simple burial boxes. The following information is intended primarily for families or groups who wish to carry out their own arrangements without a funeral director. While funeral directors ordinarily provide a casket, many will work with homemade burial boxes if requested.

Boxes of Cabinet Quality: Sometimes people buy or build nicely handcrafted boxes in advance of need to use as furniture: a settee, linen chest, or cabinet (by standing it on end with shelves inserted). Plans for making them, and in some cases the boxes as well, are available from the St. Francis Center, 5417 Sherier Pl., Washington, DC 20016, (202) 363-8500. Burial boxes are also built by Plain Pine, Harmon Road, Monterey, MA (413) 528-9937. (Free circular on request.)

Corrugated Fiber Boxes: These can be made by any firm that makes fiber boxes, but their minimum order is generally large. Many crematories and funeral directors can provide one at a cost of from $15 to $125.

Inexpensive Plywood Boxes: We offer here instructions for making four sizes of plywood boxes which are inexpensive, compact and easy to build. One group we know of keeps on hand one each of all four sizes. These boxes are not suitable for body transportation by common carrier or for keeping an unembalmed body for any length of time. If used at a funeral they may be placed on a low bench or other support and covered by a cloth (pall).

HOME-MADE BURIAL BOXES					
SIZES OF BURIAL BOXES	¾" Plywood Cheap Grade		¼" Plywood Cheap Grade		¾" Plain Lumber (or Plywood) Side Strips (2 needed)
	Bottom (1 needed)	Ends (2 needed)	Sides (2 needed)	Top (1 needed)	
LARGE SIZE Outside: 6'6" x 26" x 16" Inside: 6'4½" x 24" x 15"	6'4½" x 25½"	26" x 15¾"	6'4½" x 15¾"	6'6" x 26"	6'4½" x 5"
MEDIUM SIZE Outside: 6' x 21" x 13½" Inside: 5'10½" x 19" x 12½"	5'10½" x 20½"	21" x 13¼"	5'10½" x 13¼"	6' x 21"	5'10½" x 5"
SMALL SIZE Outside: 5'6" x 21" x 13½" Inside: 5'4½" x 19" x 12½"	5'4½" x 20½"	21" x 13¼"	5'4½" x 13¼"	5'6" x 21"	5'4½" x 4"
CHILD SIZE Outside: 3'11" x 16" x 11" Inside: 3'9½" x 14" x 10"	3'9½" x 15½"	16" x 10¾"	3'9½" x 10¾"	3'11" x 16"	3'9½" x 3"

Homemade Burial Boxes

Instructions: These four boxes can be made from two sheets of ¾"
plywood and 3½ sheets of ¼" plywood. Order the necessary parts from the
lumber yard, cut *accurately* to size. Anyone modestly experienced with tools can
assemble the boxes.

Chart for Cutting Plywood Sheets: Two sheets of ¾" 4'×8'
plywood, cut as shown in the two diagrams below, will provide all the ¾"
plywood parts needed to build the four sizes of boxes listed above. The ¼"
plywood is simpler and needs no cutting chart, so we have simply explained below
how it should be cut.

Cutting instructions for ¼" plywood: (No diagrams needed).

First Sheet (4'×8'):   Top for Large box (6'6" ×26"), and one side
(6'4½"×15¾"). Cut long way.
  Top for Child Size (3'11"×16"). Cut from remaining end.

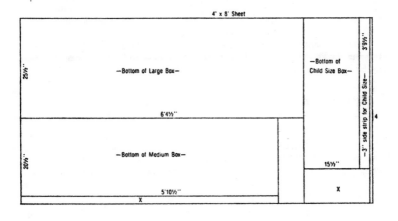

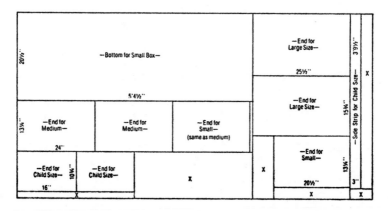

Second Sheet: Top for Medium Size (6'×21"), and two sides (5'10½" ×13¾"). Cut long way.
   Two sides for Child Size (3'9½"×10¾"). Cut from end piece.

Third Sheet: Top for Small Size (5'6"×21"), and two sides (5'4½"× 13¼"). Cut long way.
   A large end piece will be left over. This can be used to make an extra top and side of Child Size for possible future use.

Still Needed: The second side for the Large Size. If the lumber yard has part of a sheet from which this can be cut, fine. If not, a fourth sheet will be needed. In that case, the rest of the sheet can be cut into spare parts and stored with the boxes for possible later use.

Also Needed: Two side strips of ¾" lumber for Large Size (5"×6'4½").
   Two side strips of ¾" lumber for Medium Size (5"×5'10½").
   Two side strips of ¾" lumber for Small Size (4"×5'4½").
   (Side strips for Child Size were included in a previous cut.)

   From the hardware store, get some ⅞" nails, and some 4- and 8-penny box nails and four chest handles for each box. The handles should be of a kind that hang down when not in use and stay in horizontal position when lifted. Don't forget to get screws for these.

Assembly Diagram

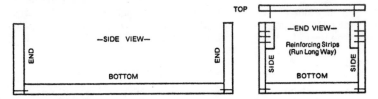

   Nail a narrow strip to each side piece, flush with the edge and the end, using 4-penny nails. The good side of the plywood should be out.
   Nail the side pieces to the bottom, using ⅞" nails. The strips should be inside and at the top.
   Nail the ends, with the good sides out, firmly to the bottom and to the side strips, using 8-penny nails, and the job is done.
   The handles may be stored inside the box and screwed on when the box is used. Likewise, the cover may be tacked lightly in place until the box is needed, and then nailed firmly down with ⅞" nails when the box is used.
   The box, when loaded, should be moved with care to avoid pulling the ends away from the box. After the cover has been nailed down, however, the box is quite strong and can be handled freely. By using screws in the ends instead of nails, the box can be made quite strong without the lid.
   When the box is used, two handles should be screwed to each end for ease in going through doors. They may be removed with a screwdriver and brought home from the crematory or cemetery for future use.
   When a body is taken to the medical school in one of these boxes, it is customary to remove the body from the box and take the box home.

To save storage space, these boxes are so designed that the medium size can nest inside the large size, and the child size inside the small size.

The design for these boxes is based, with modifications, on ones used for years by the Burial Committee of the Yellow Springs Friends Meeting. They are sturdy, inexpensive, easy to build and compact to store. Since they have been modified from the original design, we will appreciate comments and criticism from anyone who uses this design.

Burial Forms

The form shown (front and back) on the following pages was developed by the Burial Committee of the Yellow Springs (Ohio) Friends Meeting and has been in use, virtually unchanged, for thirty years. (Their term "burial" in this case is figurative. In practice the committee was concerned only with cremation or removal to a medical school.)

Each family wishing to be served by the committee was required to fill out a "Registration of Intent" for each member of the family, presumably *in advance* of need. This was done in duplicate, one copy being filed by the committee, the other retained by the family.

Very important, each family was expected to clear their plans in advance with all close relatives. Failure to do this commonly resulted in painful misunderstandings at the time of death.

About every five years the committee would review all the forms on file, to bring them up to date. The first time this was done by mailing the forms to the families asking them to update and return them. However, people don't like to think about death — especially their own — and they put off reviewing the forms, with the result that many were not returned. After that, the committee decided to update the forms by phone calls or personal visits.

The National Coalition for Fair Funeral Prices

This group originated with the Interfaith Funeral Information Committee in Phoenix, Arizona. This committee was launched in 1982 by Rev. Henry Wasielewski, pastor of the Immaculate Heart Catholic Church, and Rabbi Albert Plotkin, of Temple Beth Israel. It was promptly joined by a number of Protestant clergymen and other professionals.

A scholarly man of active social concern, Father Wasielewski had learned that some of his parishioners had paid double or more for funerals than others had paid for identical funeral services. Further investigation revealed that serious overcharging for funeral services was prevalent throughout the country — and was increasing.

To meet this problem locally, the Interfaith Committee obtained prices from all the funeral homes in the area, including some which were reasonable. This information was made available in recorded messages on two 24-hour telephone lines, one in English, one in Spanish. Persons dialing these numbers receive information on funeral costs, where to go for reasonable prices, and how to arrange for a funeral. Since these lines were installed more than 14,000 calls have been received.

As a step in making such information available in other areas the National Coalition for Fair Funeral Prices was formed, to assist groups in other places in setting up Interfaith Funeral Information Committees. In places where fair funeral prices cannot be had, the Coalition is assisting church groups in setting

REGISTRATION OF INTENT OF SIMPLE BURIAL
Yellow Springs (Ohio) Friends Meeting

THIS FORM, filled out, also includes information for obituary and legal data for death certificate.

NAME _____

Address _____

County _____ S. S. No. _____

Date of Birth _____ Place _____

Father's Name _____

Mother's Maiden Name _____

DATE FILLED OUT

DATES REVIEWED

I desire that, if circumstances permit at the time of my death, the Yellow Springs Monthly Meeting of Friends shall carry out the arrangements set forth below.

Date _____   Signature _____

Witness _____   Witness _____

☐ I wish my body cremated.
☐ I wish my body given to a medical school. (See bequeathal form)
☐ I wish my eyes given to an eye-bank.

DISPOSAL OF REMAINS: Check which of the following dispositions of ashes you request: Left at crematory for disposal there.   Delivered to one of the following:

(Names and addresses in order of preference)
FORM OF MEMORIAL SERVICE: Unless otherwise specified, the usual practice would be a memorial worship meeting at Rockford after the disposal of the body and with no expenditure for flowers. There will be no public viewing of the body. Please indicate any specific requests:

NEXT OF KIN: The following information is necessary to clear the Meeting's actions immediately on death of a participant. List next of kin in order of precedence:

NAME AND PERMANENT ADDRESS

1.

TEL.:

2.

TEL.:

3.

TEL.:

Do you expect full understanding and cooperation on the part of the above individuals?

A member of the Burial Committee will discuss with you the circumstances requiring any qualified answer.

ENDORSEMENTS: We understand and are in accord with the intent indicated above.

NAME	DATE
,	
,	

(Members of immediate family—next of kin)

FOLLOWING TO BE SIGNED AFTER DEATH OF REGISTRANT:

I authorize the Burial Committee of Yellow Springs Friends Meeting to carry out the program indicated above.

SIGNATURE:

DATE:

TWO WITNESSES:

(OVER)

BIOGRAPHICAL DATA

(Suggest pencil for items subject to change)

Marital status _____ Wedding date _____

Usual Occupation _____ Business or Industry _____

Parents' Residence (if living) _____

Sisters' & Brothers' Residences _____

_____

_____

Children's Residences _____

_____

_____

Schools attended (Dates): _____

_____

When moved here _____

Organization, community projects, special achievements _____

_____

_____

_____

(The following information is required by law for the death certificate of a veteran.)

Name of war or dates of service _____

Type of Discharge _____ Date _____ Rank _____

Service (Army, Navy, etc.) _____ Organization (Regiment, Fleet, etc.) _____

Unit (as Company, Battery, Ship, etc.) _____

Branch (Infantry, Artillery, etc.) _____

(This data may be gotten from a veteran's discharge papers.)

(OVER)

up their own mortuaries. According to Father Wasielewski this is not as difficult as one might suppose.

As a step in promoting the national organization of Interfaith Committees an advertisement similar to the one on the following page was placed in the *National Catholic Reporter,* offering to provide help in forming similar local organizations. The offer applies also to Protestant and Jewish groups, and to cooperatives. The address and phone number of the Coalition is shown in the advertisement.

The prices mentioned in this advertisement are offered by reputable funeral directors who asserted that they were making a fair profit at these rates.

Wasielewski offers a few words of counsel. Many churches and individual clergymen, he says, receive substantial support from funeral directors and as a result are reluctant to protect their parishioners from exploitative funeral prices.

Funeral directors are required by law to give price information, including response to telephone inquiries. Among the most frequently overpriced items are caskets. A casket costing the funeral director $200 may be sold to a customer for $400, $800, or even $1,200, often depending on how much the mortician thinks the customer will be able to scrape together. In asking the price of a casket it is often helpful to ask the name of the manufacturer and the model number. The Coalition can furnish wholesale price lists from most casket manufacturers, so you can find out what markup is being taken.

If a funeral director refuses to give this information, you may call the head of the Federal Trade Commission's Funeral Rule Office, Raouf Abdullah, in Washington, D.C. His number is (202) 376-2891. Mr. Abdullah encourages people to call him. The FTC will in turn call the funeral director to obtain the information. Simply telling a mortician that you will call the FTC if necessary may be sufficient to obtain the appropriate information.

Newspapers or broadcasting stations interested in making a survey of local funeral costs and practices may write to the National Coalition for Fair Funeral Prices or to the Continental Association of Funeral and Memorial Societies for advice, suggestions, videotapes of programs shown in other cities, and copies of articles published in other cities.

CHURCHES and FUNERAL PRICES

Many mortuaries and widely-advertised "pre-need" plans charge **TWO TO FIVE TIMES MORE** than is needed for a fair profit -- **overcharging families $500 to $3,000 per funeral, SERIOUSLY HARMING** many of your families and senior citizens.

Here are FAIR PRICES currently charged by mortuaries in a number of U.S. communities -- possible by mortuaries in most communities:

> ### COMPLETE TRADITIONAL FUNERAL
> **$840-1100 (without casket)**
>
> ### METAL CASKETS (many attractive styles, colors)
> **$275-500**
>
> ### CREMATION (mortuary & crematory total)
> **$275-450**

CLERGY and CONCERNED CITIZENS: Phone several mortuaries in your area for their lowest prices for each of the above. **If they charge more than these prices, your community has a problem.**

YOU CAN HELP YOUR FAMILIES: Contact us for a kit explaining **how to help your people obtain fair mortuary and cemetery prices** and refunds on pre-pay plans and past funerals. Information about: pre-pay and insurance plans, deceptive practices, federal regulations, advice of national consumer agencies, casket wholesale prices (now available for the first time in the U.S.), price lists of fair-priced mortuaries, how local churches and groups have started 24-hour price "hotlines" and fair-priced mortuaries. ($4)

YOUR CHURCH can easily cause local mortuaries to lower their prices to FAIR levels, helping all families in the community, especially if you invite other churches and community groups to join in these simple steps: **1)** Regularly publish the fair-price list above, together with the names/prices of your neighborhood mortuaries for the same items, and names/prices of the lowest-priced firms you find in your area and in nearby communities. Ask mortuaries with high prices to **explain** why. **2)** Regularly urge all families to avoid mortuaries with unfair prices. Urge families to use church facilities for visitation and all funeral services so that they aren't forced to use chapels of high-priced mortuaries nearby. Mortuaries will lower their prices because of the shame of price exposure and loss of business. **3)** To avoid giving the impression that your church approves of the high prices of mortuaries, and unfair contracts and prices of most pre-pay plans, do not distribute advertising calendars of high-priced mortuaries and remove promotional inserts of plans. Other businesses with fair prices will sponsor calendars.

NOW AVAILABLE: Videotape of U.S. TV stations' investigative reports of abuses and overcharges by local mortuaries and pre-pay plans. ($10 postpaid) Show to church and civic groups to help them protect themselves. Give a copy to your TV stations and newspapers and urge them to check on unjust prices and sales methods in your area.

NATIONAL COALITION
FOR FAIR FUNERAL PRICES
P.O. Box 2266, Phoenix, AZ 85002 -- (602) 838-0297

Duplicate this for clergy, church groups, and agencies concerned about families.

APPENDIX 6 / *Directory of Memorial Societies*

Continental Association of Funeral and Memorial Societies (CAFMS), 7910 Woodmont Ave., Suite 1208, Bethesda, MD 20814-3015 (301) 913-0030. (See also Chapter 6, "Memorial Societies.")

Publications of CAFMS

The American Way of Death, Jessica Mitford. Fawcett Crest, 1979, 288 pp. $5.00. Updated version of 1963 classic.

"Directory of Memorial Societies in US and Canada." Single copies free.

"Facts about Cremation." Fact sheet, single copies free.

Forms for Bequeathal to medical school. $2.00.

Handbook for Funeral & Memorial Societies. CAFMS, 1976, 100 pp. $10.00. Essential how-to-do-it guide for organizing & running a memorial society.

"How to Organize a Memorial - Funeral Society." Leaflet, single copies free.

A Multitude of Voices: Funerals & the Clergy. Packet for leaders of all religious faiths. Includes booklet of funeral information, sample insert for Sunday/Sabbath bulletin or separate distribution, sample copy of "Smoothing the Way" guide & form for funeral planning, directory of memorial societies, poster for display. $1.50.

"Putting My House in Order." Four-page form for listing all estate and funeral planning information needed by a person's heirs at time of death. $1.00.

Uniform Donor Cards. Single cards free.

"What Everyone Should Know about Funeral and Memorial Planning." $1.00

Ordering Information

Make check or money order payable to "Memorial Society Fund." Payment must accompany order. Bulk prices available on request. Allow 4–6 weeks for delivery. For single copy request please enclose a self-addressed, stamped business-size envelope.

Directory of Funeral and Memorial Societies

Memorial Societies of Canada

ALBERTA: *Calgary:* Calgary Co-op Memorial Society, 28 Norseman Pl., N.W., T2K 5M6   (403) 274-5120

Edmonton: Memorial Society of Edmonton & District, 3516 - 13th Ave., T6L 3B3   (403) 474-0414

Red Deer: Memorial Society of Red Deer & District, P.O. Box 817, T4N 5H2   (403) 340-1021

BR. COLUMBIA: *Vancouver:* Memorial Society of B.C., 410 - 207 West Hastings St., V6B 1J3   (604) 688-6256

MANITOBA: *Winnipeg:* Manitoba Funeral Planning and Memorial Society, 790 Banning St., R3E 2H9 (204) 783-8312

NEW BRUNSWICK: *Fredericton:* Memorial Society of New Brunswick, Box 622, E3B 5A6

Moncton: Memorial Society of New Brunswick, Inc., P.O. Box 1013, E1C 8P2(506) 855-8176/8792

Saint John: Memorial Society of New Brunswick, Inc., P.O.Box 6242, Station A, E2L 4R7

NEWFOUNDLAND: *St. John's:* Mem. and Funeral Planning Soc. of Nfld., Box 9183, Station B, A1A 2X9   (709) 368-7784/5539

NOVA SCOTIA: *Halifax:* Greater Halifax Memorial Society, P.O. Box 56, Lower Sackville, B4C 2S8   (902) 865-5370

Sydney: Memorial Society of Cape Breton, P.O. Box 934, B1P 6J4   (902) 539-6536

ONTARIO: *Belleville:* Mem. Soc. of Quinte, P.O. Box 477, K8N 5B2 (613) 968-7640

Guelph: Memorial Society of Guelph, P.O.Box 1784, N1H 7A1 (519) 822-7430

Hamilton: Hamilton Mem. Soc., P.O. Box 164, Station A, L8N 3A2 (416) 549-6385

Kingston: Mem. Soc. of Kingston, P.O. Box 1081, K7L 4Y5 (613) 544-4438

Kitchener: Kitchener-Waterloo Memorial Society, P.O. Box 113, Sta. C, N2G 3W9   (519) 576-1265/699-4028

London: Memorial Society of London, P.O. Box 1729, Sta. A, N6A 5H9 (519) 472-0670

Niagara Falls: Niagara Peninsula Memorial Society, P.O. Box 2102, 4500 Queen St., L2E 6Z2 (416) 358-5060

Ottawa: Ottawa Memorial Society, 1162 Rockingham Ave.,   K1H 8A7 (613) 523-0491

Peterborough: Funeral Planning Association (Memorial Society) of Peterborough & District, P.O. Box 1795, K9J 7X6   (705) 742-0550

Sudbury: Memorial Society of Northern Ontario, Box 2563, Sta. A, P3A 4S9   (705) 673-5532

Thunder Bay: Memorial Society of Thunder Bay, P.O. Box 501, Sta. F, P7C 4W4   (807) 683-3051

Toronto: Toronto Memorial Society, P.O. Box 96, Sta. A, Weston, M9N 3M6 (416) 241-6274

Windsor: Mem. Soc. of Windsor & Dist., P.O. Box 481, N9A 6M6   (519) 566-1064/969-6767

QUEBEC: *Montreal:* L'Association Funeraire de Montreal/Mem.Assoc. of Montreal, Box 802, Sta. "C" H2L 4L6 (514) 521-2815

SASKATCHEWAN: *Lloydminster:* Lloyd

minster, Vermillion & District Mem. Soc., P.O. Box 1008, 4805 - 47th St., S9V 0K2   (306) 825-3769
   Saskatoon: Memorial Society of Saskatchewan, P.O. Box 1846, S7K 3S2 (306) 374-5190

Continental Association of Funeral & Memorial Societies

ALASKA: *Anchorage:* Cook Inlet Memorial Society, Box 10-2414   95510 (907) 272-7801/277-6001

ARIZONA: *Phoenix:* Valley Memorial Society, P.O. Box 3074, Scottsdale 85257   (602) 990-3055
   Prescott: Memorial Society of Prescott, 335 E. Aubrey St.   86303 (602) 778-3000
   Tucson: Tucson Mem. Soc., Box 12661 85732-2661 (602) 721-0230
   Yuma: Mem. Society of Yuma, Box 4314   85364   (602) 726-8014

ARKANSAS: *Fayetteville:* Northwest Arkansas Memorial Society, P.O.Box 3055   72702   (501) 433-1404
   Little Rock: Memorial Society of Central Arkansas, 12213 Rivercrest Dr.   72212   (501) 225-7276

CALIFORNIA:*Bakersfield* Kern Memorial Society, P.O. Box 1201   93302-1202   (806) 831-6176/366-7266
   Berkeley: Bay Area Funeral Soc., Box 264   947012   (415) 841-6653
   Eureka: Humboldt Funeral Society, P.O. Box 6036 95502 (707) 822-2445
   Fresno: Valley Memorial Society, Box 101   93707   (209) 268-2181
   Los Angeles: Los Angeles Funeral Society, Inc., P.O. Box 92313, Pasadena 91109-2313   (818) 791-4829 (Hotline 791-2060)
   Modesto: Stanislaus Mem. Soc., Box 4252   95352   (209) 523-0316
   Palo Alto: Peninsula Funeral and Memorial Society, Box 60448   94306 (415) 321-2109
   Sacramento: Sacramento Valley Memorial Society, Inc., Box 161688, 3720 Folsom Blvd. 95816 (916) 451-4641

   San Diego: San Diego Mem. Soc., Box 16336 92116-0336 (619) 293-0928
   San Luis Obispo: Central Coast Memorial Society, Box 679   93406 (805) 543-6133
   Santa Barbara: Channel Cities Memorial Society, Box 424   93102 (805) 569-1794
   Santa Cruz: Funeral & Memorial Society of Monterey Bay, Inc., Box 2900 95063   (408) 462-6832/462-1333
   Stockton San Joaquin Mem. Soc., Box 4832   95204   (209) 466-7743

COLORADO: *Denver:* Rocky Mountain Memorial Society, 4101 E. Hampden Ave.   80222   (303) 759-2800

CONNECTICUT: *Westport:* Memorial Society Of S.W. Connecticut, 71 Hillendale Rd.   06880   (203) 227-8705

DISTRICT OF COLUMBIA: *Washington:* Memorial Society of Metro. Washington, 1500 Harvard St., N.W. 20009 (202) 234-7777

FLORIDA: *Cocoa:* Funeral & Memorial Society of Brevard County Inc., Box 276   32923-0276   (407) 453-4109/ 783-7907
   DeBary: Funeral Soc., of Mid-Florida, Box 262 32713 (407) 668-5963
   Ft. Myers: Funeral & Mem. Soc., of S.W. Florida, Inc., P.O. Box 7756 33911 (813) 939-3368
   Ft. Walton Beach: Memorial Society of Northwest Florida, P.O.Box 4122 32549-4122   (904) 651-3118
   Gainesville: Memorial Society of Alachua County, P.O. Box 14662 32604 (904) 332-5934

Miami: Miami Memorial Society, 115 Country Club Prado   Coral Gables 33134   (305) 266-1403

Orlando: The Memorial & Funeral Soc. of Greater Orlando, Inc., c/o First Unitarian Church, 1815 E. Robinson St. 32803 (407) 898-3621/647-0631

Pensacola: Funeral & Memorial Soc. of Pensacola & West Florida, P.O. Drawer 18485 32523 (904) 932-9566/ 477-8431/482-8893

St. Petersburg: Suncoast-Tampa Bay Memorial Soc., 719 Arlington Ave. N. 33701   (813) 898-3294

Sarasota: Memorial Society of Sarasota, Box 15833   34277   (813) 953-3740/957-3093

Tallahassee: Funeral & Memorial Society of Leon County, 1006 Buena Vista Dr.   32304

Tampa: Tampa Memorial Society, 3915 N. "A" St.   33609 (813) 877-4604

W. Palm Beach: Palm Beach Funeral Soc., Box 2065 33402 (407) 833-8936

GEORGIA: *Atlanta:* Memorial Society of Georgia, 1911 Cliff Valley Way, N.E. 30329   (404) 634-2896

HAWAII: *Honolulu:* Memorial Soc. of Hawaii, 2510 Bingham St. NE, Room A 96826   (808) 946-6822

IDAHO: *Boise:* Idaho Memorial Assn., P.O. Box 1919 83701 (208) 343-1139

ILLINOIS: *Chicago:* Chicago Memorial Association, 5032 Blackstone   60615 (312) 939-0678

Urbana: Champaign County Memorial Society, 309 W. Green St.   61801 (217) 384-8862

INDIANA: *Bloomington:* Bloomington Memorial Society, 2120 N. Fee Lane 47401   (812) 332-3695

Ft. Wayne: Northeastern Indiana Memorial Society, Inc., 2923 Woodstock Court   46815   (219) 484-4385

Indianapolis: Indianapolis Memorial Society, 5805 E. 56th St.   46226 (317) 545-6005/844-1371

Valparaiso: Memorial Society of Northwest Indiana, 356 McIntyre Ct. 46383   (219) 462-5701

West Lafayette: Memorial Society of Mid North Indiana, Inc., Box 2155 47906   (317) 463-9645

IOWA: *Ames:* Central Iowa Mem. Soc., 1015 Hyland Ave. 50010 (515) 239-2314

Davenport: Illowa Memorial Funeral Society, 1609 Lincoln Rd., Bettendorf 52722   (319) 355-3043

Iowa City: Memorial Society of Iowa River Valley, 120 N. Dubuque St. 52245   (319) 337-3019/5989

KENTUCKY: *Lexington:* Memorial Soc. of Lexington, Inc., 3564 Clays Mill Rd. 40503   (606) 223-1448

Louisville: Memorial Society of Greater Louisville, c/o Spragens, 891 Minona Ave.   40117   (502)637-5911

LOUISIANA: *Baton Rouge:* Memorial Soc. of Greater Baton Rouge, 8470 Goodwood Ave. 70806 (504) 926-2291

MAINE: *Auburn:* Mem. Soc. of Maine, Box 3122 04212-3122 (207) 786-4323

MARYLAND: *Bethesda:* Memorial Society of Maryland, 9601 Cedar Lane 20814 (301) 564-0006

MASSACHUSETTS: *Brewster:* Memorial Society of Cape Cod, c/o Frank Kynor, Box 404   02631   (508)896-3370

Brockton: Memorial Soc. of Greater Brockton, 325 W. Elm St.   02401 (508) 583-7775

Brookline: Memorial Society of New England, 25 Monmouth St. 02146 (617) 731-2073

New Bedford: Memorial Society of Southeastern MA, Inc., 71 Eighth St. 02740   (508) 994-9686

Springfield: Springfield Memorial Society, Box 2821 01101 (413) 783-7987

MICHIGAN: *Ann Arbor:* Memorial Advisory & Planning Svc., 2030 Chaucer 48103   (313) 665-9516

Battle Creek: Mem. Soc. of Battle Creek, c/o Art Center, 265 E. Emmet St. 49017   (616) 962-5362

Detroit: Greater Detroit Memorial Society, P.O. Box 1321   Royal Oak 48068   (313) 547-1330

East Lansing: Lansing Area Memorial Planning Society, 765 Collingwood   48823   (517) 351-3988

Flint: Mem. Soc. of Flint, P.O.Box 4315   48504   (313) 239-2596

Grand Rapids: Mem. Soc. of Greater Grand Valley, Box 1426   49501

Mt. Pleasant: Mem. Soc. of Mid-Michigan, 1307 East High   48858 (517) 773-9548

MINNESOTA: *Minneapolis/St. Paul:* Minnesota Funeral & Memorial Society, c/o Lindquist, 2185 Carter Ave., St. Paul 55108   (612) 647-9861

Outside Minneapolis: 717 Riverside Dr. SE, St. Cloud 56301 (612) 252-7540

MISSISSIPPI: *Biloxi:* Fun. & Mem. Soc. of the Miss. Gulf Coast, 1736 William Harrison Drive 39531 (601) 435-2284

MISSOURI: *Kansas City:* Greater Kansas City Memorial Society, 4500 Warwick Blvd.   64111   (816) 531-1740

St. Louis: Memorial & Planned Funeral Society, 5007 Waterman Blvd.   63108   (314) 361-0595

MONTANA: *Billings:* Memorial Society of Montana, 1024 Princeton Ave. 59102   (406) 252-5065/1828

Missoula: Five Valleys Burial Memorial Association, 406 University Ave.   59801   (406) 543-6952

NEBRASKA: *Omaha:* Midland Memorial Society, 3114 Harney St.   68131 (402) 345-3039

NEVADA: *Las Vegas:* Funeral & Mem. Soc. of S. Nevada, Inc., P.O. Box 60891 89160   (702) 739-6979

Reno: Mem. Soc. of Western Nev., Box 8413, University Station   89507 (702) 852-4600

New Hampshire: *Concord:* Mem. Soc. of New Hampshire, Box 702   03302-1176 (603) 224-8913

NEW JERSEY: *Cherry Hill:* Mem. Soc. of South Jersey, 401 King's Hwy. N. 08034   (609) 667-3618/866-0597

East Brunswick: Raritan Valley Memorial Society, 176 Tices Lane 08816   (201) 246-9620/572-1470

Lincroft: Memorial Association of Monmouth County, 1475 W. Front St. 07738   (201) 747-0707

Madison: Morris Memorial Society, Box 156   07940   (201) 540-1177

Montclair: Memorial Society of Essex, Box 888, Upper Montclair 07043   (201) 783-1145

Paramus: Central Mem. Society, 156 Forest Ave. 07652 (201) 836-7267

Plainfield: Mem. Soc. of Plainfield, 858 Princeton Ct. Branchburg 08853

Princeton: Princeton Mem. Assn., Inc., 48 Roper Rd. 08540 (609) 924-1604/924-1604

NEW MEXICO: *Albuquerque:* Memorial Assn. of Central N.M., Box 3251 87190

Las Cruces: Mem. & Fun. Soc. of Southern NM, P.O. Box 6531   88006 (505) 526-6899

Santa Fe: Mem. & Fun. Soc. of Northern NM, P.O. Box 4637 87502 (505) 983-3135

NEW YORK: *Albany:* Mem. Soc. of the Hudson Mohawk Reg., 405 Washington Ave.   12206-2604   (518) 465-9664

Binghamton: Southern Tier Mem. Soc. 183 Riverside 13905 (607) 770-4722

Buffalo: Greater Buffalo Mem. Soc., 695 Elmwood 14222 (716) 885-2136

Corning: Memorial Society of Greater Corning, Box 23, Painted Post 14870   (607) 962-7132/936-6563

Hornell: Upper Genesee Memorial Society, 335 S. Main St.   Alfred 14802   (607) 587-8429

Ithaca: Ithaca Mem. Soc., Box 134 14851   (607) 273-8316

New Hartford: Mohawk Valley Mem. Soc., PO Box 322 13413 (315) 797-1955

N.Y.C.: Community Church Funeral Soc., 40 E. 35th St. 10016 (212) 683-4988

N.Y.C.: Memorial Soc. of Riverside Church, 490 Riverside Dr. 10027 (212) 222-5900 × 258

Pomona: Rockland Co. Mem. Soc., Box 461   10970   (914) 354-2917

Port Washington: Memorial Society of Long Island, Inc., Box 303   11050 (516) 627-6590/944-9035

Poughkeepsie: Mid-Hudson Memorial Society, 249 Hooker Ave.   12603 (914) 462-3309

Rochester: Rochester Mem. Soc., 220 Winton Rd. S. 14610 (716) 461-1620

Syracuse: Syracuse Mem. Soc., Box 67, Dewitt 13214-0067 (315) 474-4580

Watertown: Memorial Society of Northern New York, c/o Schwerzmann, 1138 Harrison St. 13601 (315) 788-6700

White Plains: Funeral Planning Assn. of Westchester, Rosedale Ave. & Sycamore Lane   10605   (914) 946-1660

NORTH CAROLINA: *Asheville:* Blue Ridge Memorial Society, Box 2601 28802   (704) 669-2587

Chapel Hill: Triangle Memorial & Funeral Society, Box 1223   27514 (919) 942-4427

Greensboro: Piedmont Mem. & Fun. Soc., Box 16192   27406 (919) 674-5501

Laurinburg: Scotland Co. Funeral & Mem. Soc., Box 192 28352 (919) 276-7099/2119

Wilmington: Memorial Society of the Lower Cape Fear, P.O. Box 4262 28406   (919) 762-5252

OHIO: *Akron:* Memorial Society of Akron Canton, 3300 Morewood Rd. 44313   (216) 836-2206

Cincinnati: Memorial Society of Greater Cincinnati, Inc., 536 Linton St. 45219   (513) 281-1564

Cleveland: Cleveland Memorial Society, 21600 Shaker Blvd.   Shaker Heights 44122   (216) 751-5515

Columbus: Mem. Soc. of the Columbus Area, 93 W. Weisheimer Rd., P.O. Box 14385   43214   (614) 267-4946

Dayton: Dayton Mem. Soc., 665 Salem Ave.   45406   (513) 274-5890

Toledo: Memorial Society of Northwest Ohio, 610 Stickney Ave., #2809   43604   (419) 729-4437

Wilmington: Funeral & Memorial Society of Southwest Ohio, 66 N. Mulberry St.   45177   (513) 382-2349

Yellow Springs: Yellow Springs Branch of Memorial Society of Columbus Area, 317 Dayton St.   45387 (513) 767-1659

Youngstown: Memorial Society of Greater Youngstown, 75 Jackson Drive, Campbell   44405   (216) 755-8696

OREGON: *Eugene:* The Emerald Mem. Assn., PO Box 11347, Pleasant Hill 97440

Portland: Oregon Memorial Assn., 811 E. Burnside, Ste. 122 97214 (503) 239-0150

PENNSYLVANIA: *Bethlehem:* Lehigh Valley Mem. Soc., 701 Lechauweki Ave. 18015   (215) 866-7652

Erie: Thanatopsis Society of Erie, Box 3495   16508   (814) 864-9300

Harrisburg: Memorial Society of Greater Harrisburg, 1280 Clover Lane 17113   (717) 564-4761

Philadelphia: Memorial Society of Greater Philadelphia, 2125 Chestnut Street   19103   (215) 567-1065

Pittsburgh: Pittsburgh Mem. Soc., 605 Morewood   15213 (412) 621-4740

Pottstown: Pottstown Branch of Mem. Soc. of Greater Philadelphia, 1409 N. State St. 19464 (215) 323-5561

State College: Mem. Soc. of Central Pennsylvania, 758 Glenn Road 16803 (814) 237-7605

Wilkes-Barre: Mem. Soc. of Northeast PA, P.O. Box 2216,   18703-2216

RHODE ISLAND: *East Greenwich:* Mem. Soc. of Rhode Island, 119 Kenyon Ave.   02818   (401) 884-5933

TENNESSEE: *Chattanooga:* Memorial Society of Chattanooga, 3224 Navajo Dr.   37411   (615) 899-9315

Knoxville: East Tenn. Mem. Soc., Box 10507 37939 (615) 523-4176
Nashville: Middle Tenn. Mem. Soc., 1808 Woodmont 37215 (615) 383-5760
Pleasant Hill: Cumberland Branch of East Tennessee Mem. Soc., Box 246 38578 (615) 277-3795

TEXAS: *Austin:* Austin Mem. & Burial Information Soc., Box 4382 78765 (512) 477-5238
Dallas: Dallas Area Mem. Soc., 4015 Normandy 75205 (214) 528-6006
El Paso: Mem. Soc. of El Paso, Box 4951 79914 (505) 824-4565/542-0812
Houston: Houston Area Mem. Soc., 5210 Fannin St. 77004 (713) 526-4267
Lubbock: Lubbock Area Mem. Soc., Box 6562 79413
San Antonio: San Antonio Memorial Society, 807 Beryl Drive 78213 (512) 341-2213

UTAH: *Salt Lake City:* Utah Mem. Assn., 569 S. 1300 East 84102 (801) 582-8687

VERMONT: *Burlington:* Vermont Mem. Soc., Box 67 05401 (802) 863-4701

VIRGINIA: *Alexandria:* Mt. Vernon Mem. Soc., 1909 Windmill Lane 22307 (703) 765-5950

Arlington: Mem. Soc. of Northern Va., 4444 Arlington Blvd. 22204 (703) 271-9240
Charlottesville: Memorial Planning Society of the Piedmont, 717 Rugby Rd. 22903 (804) 293-8179
Richmond: Memorial Society of Greater Richmond, P.O. Box 29315 23229 (804) 285-9157/355-0777
Salem: Roanoke Valley Mem. Soc., 2152 Bainbridge Drive 24153
Virginia Beach: Mem. Soc. of Tidewater, Box 4621 23454 (804) 481-2991

WASHINGTON: *Seattle:* People's Mem. Assn., 2366 Eastlake Ave. E. 98102 (206) 325-0489
Spokane: Spokane Mem. Assn., Box 13613 99213 (509) 924-8400
Yakima: Mem. Soc. of Central Wash. P.O. Box 379 98907 (509) 452 -1712

WISCONSIN: *Egg Harbor:* Mem. Soc. of Wisconsin (also, Mem. Soc. of Door County), 6900 Lost Lake Road 54209 (414) 868-3136
Madison: Mem. Soc. of Madison, 5235 Harbor Ct. MN 53705 (608) 238-4422
Milwaukee: Fun. & Mem. Soc. of Greater Milwaukee, 8801 W. Libson 53222 (414) 962-0400
Racine: Mem. Soc. of SE Wisconsin, 625 College Ave. 53403 (414) 634-0659

APPENDIX 7 / *Sample Death Ceremonies*

Editor's Note: Most religious traditions include death services. The ceremonies in this appendix supplement these traditional services.

Memorial Services

On the following pages are several memorial services, each of which has been selected for some feature that seemed especially interesting. They have been compiled by Ann Baty of the Bowling Green, Ohio Memorial Society. Each of the first seven was written for a particular person who had died. Of the others, one is a general type of service that can be used for anyone. It is followed by two committal services — one for burial and one for cremation. The children's "Good-bye Service" is not intended for a formal service but is meant to be used to help a child or children to cope with a grievous loss.

I. Service with Flower Communion

The memorial service for Esme Harold Naaman was prepared by a friend. Esme's death had ended several months of loving care given by friends who made it possible for him to die at home.

An order of service was mimeographed and folded into a booklet of ten pages plus cover. It contained the full text of all the selections that were used. It was mailed to friends and family who could not attend and served, for some, as a notice of Esme's death. The cover had his name and the dates of his birth and death with a paragraph about the kind of person he was.

After an interval of music by Bach and Brahms, as people gathered, the service began with these words: "We are a group of friends gathered together to pay loving tribute to Esme Naaman and to share with his family and each other our appreciation of a rare and remarkable human being."

Words written about him by a friend or two were read, as were a couple of letters that he had received (from brother and son) and which contained revealing sentiments. There were other readings: from *Voice of the Desert* by Joseph Wood Krutch, from *The Prophet* by Kahlil Gibran and from Kenneth L. Patton. There were intervals of music (Sibelius, Croft, Mozart, Bach) and a short eulogy. A statement of the kind of person Esme had been was read by the minister.

Finally a friend said, "We invite you to take a blossom in our diverse remembrances of Esme." To the accompaniment of Bach's "Vater Unser in Himmelriech," four friends passed shallow baskets of chrysanthemum blossoms

127

in yellow, bronze and white as a flower communion; after that was a recitation of The Lord's Prayer and then a recessional by Bach.

The service was held in a Unitarian Church but was conducted by lay friends, rather than by the minister. The selections written by Kenneth L. Patton were *The Measure of Sorrow* and *Our Own Good-Byes*.

II. Service Using Writings of the Deceased

Marcos Romero was a very creative young man from South America. While attending college in the United States, he was killed in a motorcycle accident. His friends put together this memorial service, using Marcos' own writings. The short service was held in a room in one of the college halls, and it was conducted entirely by students, his friends.

A program was printed and titled "Remembering Marcos Romero, A service of Readings and Reflections." Date and place of the service also were printed on the cover.

The service began with a reading by a friend, followed by this litany:

LOVE ONE ANOTHER
Support one another's efforts
LOVE ONE ANOTHER
Rejoice in another's fulfillment
LOVE ONE ANOTHER
Support each other through difficult times
LOVE ONE ANOTHER
Rejoice together in times of rejoicing
LOVE ONE ANOTHER

Friends read from Marcos' writings, then sang a song written for Marcos by a friend. "Morning Has Broken" was sung by the group (the words were printed on the program).

There was a benediction from Marcos' writings "Life is a matter of doing whatever has to be done with as much love as possible. By love, I mean concentration and dedication of one's life. I find that it is not so important to plan for the future, but to love everything we do and to let go and flow as a river flows."

The service ended with the reading of a poem written by Marcos Romero, titled "Good-bye: Dedicated to All Those Friends of Mine Who Listen."

III. Service with Organ Music

This service was arranged by friends of the deceased and was conducted by them. Harold Thomas Marlow had cared for his mother for many years until she died; he never married. After his mother died, he spent his time and energy working for his church; he left everything he had to the church.

The church had an organ and an organist, and most of the music was played by the organist. The service:

Prelude   Trumpet Tune in C and Trumpet Tune in D
—Purcell

Opening Words   "Reasons for a Funeral or Memorial
Service"   *—Rev. Roy Phillips*

We do best in our present and later lives if, when one we love dies, we bring together those whose lives were touched significantly by the life of the one who has died. This is the reason for a funeral or a memorial service.

While such services have been understood in many varying ways, their human function is to set an experiential marker at the endpoint of life, to place a cairn at the conclusion of one human being's journey.

The cairns along a wilderness trail are built of earth rocks of various shapes and sizes. The memorial cairn at the end of a life is also a composite, but an experiential one. It is made up of the memories, the thoughts and the feelings of all who are gathered in the one place together. It is a recollection (a re-collection) of what was for a time together and is now scattered and scattering. Here is the one we knew. This is how our lives were touched by that life. Here is what we think and how we feel.

The words spoken in the literal funeral or memorial service are not themselves the marker. The spoken words are evokers of experiences — thoughts, feelings, memories — within the people of the gathered group. These experiences are the memorial cairn.

At the end of a life, we compose a symphony, an ordered creation whose notes and themes are the experiences of the people gathered. Themes dark and bright are sounded to recollect and to order the impact of the life of the one who had died — honestly, fully, tenderly — and in the spirit of thanksgiving for the quality of that lived life.

The words of a memorial service should strive to evoke remembrance, thanksgiving, a sense of the uniqueness of the person's life, a sense of the privilege of having known that person, a sense of loss, of sadness, a feeling of emptiness, of unsureness and a hint that the ending of this life is a rehearsal of what is to come for every one of us. The words should evoke a sense of trust in the slow, but steady, grace of healing and the affirmation that we can live on and will live on, blessed by that life and by the memory of the one who once was and is now gone, but who is and will be present in the world, and in us in mysterious and hidden ways.

> Harold Thomas Marlow, scholar, churchman, friend, has died. We are gathered here to pay honor to his spirit and to the life he lived, and to consecrate his memory. The readings and music speak of him; reflect his spirit in life; reflect our feeling for him, and our feeling at this time.

Introit   "Well-Tempered Clavichord"   — *Bach*

Readings "A Celebration for George Sarton" (final stanza)
                                                            — *May Sarton*

              "On Death"   — *Kahlil Gibran*

Solo   "Jesu, Joy of Man's Desiring"   — *Bach*

Invitation to Thought

(Words about Tom spoken by the minister, and ending with a short meditation)

Do you seek Tom Marlow? Why seek ye the living among the dead? All tombs are empty, signposts toward the silent mystery that is our origin and destiny. Seek the living among the living. Seek Tom in yourselves, in the patterns of your mind and memory, in the shape of the world made a little different by him, in the very rhythm of your heart of hearts. Amen.

Solo   "Pathetique Sonata Andante Cantabile"
                                              —Beethoven

Eulogy   (read by a boyhood friend)
Solo   "Für Elise"   *—Beethoven*
Reading   "There Are Men Too Gentle to Live Among Wolves"*
                                              —James Kavanaugh

Music   "Suite in C"   *—Bach*
Closing Words
    We, the living, have come together to ponder the death of one known to us, loved by us. We have come with sorrow that a good life should have to end. We have come with deep memories of our times with him, of joy and sorrow we shared with him, of the delightful and even the impatient moments we knew when he was with us. Here was a man, a man with hopes and dreams; a man with secret fears and unanswered questions; but a man with a zest for life and the strength to weather the storms which each of us must face. We, the living, give thanks that we have known Tom. We give thanks that he walked among us. We give thanks that he lived. Amen.

Postlude "St. Anthony Chorale"   *—Haydn-Brahms*

Sources

The readings suggested in this service can be found in the following sources: May Sarton, *Collected Poems: 1930-1973,* Norton, 1974; Kahlil Gibran, *The Prophet,* Alfred A. Knopf; James Kavanaugh, *There Are Men too Gentle to Live Among Wolves,* Dutton, 1970.

IV. Service Held for a Teen-Aged Girl

Mary, sixteen, was killed while on vacation with her family. Her body was cremated with a private committal service.

When the family returned to their home, a memorial service was held in the United Methodist Church to which they belonged. Significant objects relating to Mary, things she prized, graced the chancel area.

Music significant to the family, including "Bridge Over Troubled Water," was played.

The pastor spoke sentences of hope and comfort from the Scriptures, and he read the Twenty-Third Psalm. He prayed, and the congregation prayed The Lord's Prayer in unison. They sang "Precious Lord."

The youth minister read portions of the eighth chapter of Romans and preached on the text, "The Spirit Himself Intercedes for Us with Sighs Too Deep for Words."

A friend sang "One Day at a Time."

Those present were invited to share their thoughts about Mary with one

---

*Our apologies to the four-legged wolves. They are not the ones referred to in this poem. As Farley Mowatt says, "Never Cry Wolf" — unless you specify which kind.

another as the spirit moved them. (Mary's high school English teacher read from Mary's writings. One of her brothers read a poem she had written. Her father and mother, referring to the objects in the room and recent conversations with Mary, expressed their grief and hope and their need for the community of love.)

The congregation sang "Joy Is Like the Rain."

They were invited to come forward and stand with family for Holy communion. The minister took the bread and a cup, gave thanks, broke the bread—a loaf baked by a friend—and gave the bread and the cup to the people, who served one another hand to hand.

They sang "Amazing Grace," received the benediction, and sang "Shalom-"—the congregation's customary closing song. The people spontaneously shared their love with the family, and then gradually dispersed.

—from *Abingdon Funeral Manual* by Perry H. Biddle, Jr.
Quoted with permission, Abingdon Press, Nashville TN

V. A Memorial Walk

A "Memorial Walk" was held for Steve Persons on a Sunday afternoon at the small golf course in the Mobile Home Park where he had been living. Steve had been an avid golfer for many years and many friends knew him best in the golf setting.

Steve's friends gathered at the designated entrance to a path that followed the edge of the greens toward the Mobile Home Park club house just two short blocks away. The family arrived and led the group along the path to a midpoint bordering the golf course, where a large oak tree spread its branches. Here they stopped. Some sat on a bench beneath the tree as the friends grouped themselves around the family. While those in attendance absorbed the beauty of the golf course where Steve had spent so many happy hours, his nephew spoke some words of greeting, then gave a biographical sketch of Steve's life. Two of Steve's favorite songs were played on a cassette tape recorder, after which a friend spoke briefly and respectfully about Steve's interests and accomplishments in the world of music. The family then led the walk to the club house entrance where they turned and greeted their friends who passed through the door into the building.

Inside, the group found seats in the informal lounge. Simple refreshments were served while favorite classical piano selections were played. People were able to relax comfortably to talk to each other and the family, and especially to talk with relatives from afar whom they had not seen for a long time.

This memorial service, though quite simple, was very comforting and filled with love. Real support and sympathy was shown to the family as they and their friends exchanged incidents, anecdotes and many remembrances about their beloved Steve throughout the rest of the afternoon.

VI. An Unstructured Service Held in a Farmyard

This was a service held for Tom Blank. He had grown up on a farm near a small city. He had lived in the same community all of his life. After he died, his brother arranged for a memorial service held outdoors in the farmyard, just as Tom once, years before, had said he'd like it to be.

Chairs were carried out onto the lawn; a table of soft drinks was set up at one side. A rowboat that Tom had enjoyed using on the river in his playtime hours was filled with garden and field flowers; it also held a self-portrait Tom had painted.

There were some prepared readings, but guests were invited to, and did, speak as the spirit moved them to do so about their love for Tom.

VII. A Quaker Service

A man describes the unplanned service for his wife as "The most beautiful and meaningful memorial service I ever attended."

She had become a very active and devoted Friend (Quaker) after having been a Catholic for more than sixty years. She died very early on a Saturday morning. A friend of hers went all over the campus (where they taught) and spread the word to all her friends, asking them to attend the regular Sunday morning service of the Friends Meeting — even if they were not Quakers. And they did. "In the traditional Quaker manner," the gentleman writes, "all sat around in a circle with only a rug and a large candle in the center, and a number of those who knew her spoke feelingly of what she had meant to them, and what she had done for other people. There were no rehearsed speeches, no eulogy by someone who had to be briefed. The testimonies were given from firsthand experience and from the heart ... and at the end, all joined hands with their neighbors, in accordance with their custom."

VIII. Love Memorial for Our Son (as described by his mother)

Scott had been a skydiver for ten years, with over 2,000 jumps and twenty-four hours of freefall. His skydiving had taken him all over the United States and Europe. He had always assured me, when I worried, that he was safer in the air than driving on the highway.

We were totally unprepared, therefore, for the news of his death 1,000 miles away from home. We didn't know what to do. We were aware of the local Memorial Society; we weren't members, but we knew people who were. We called them and got the telephone number of the Memorial Society in Tampa, where Scott had been killed. We called there, and they put us in touch with a funeral home. Scott's body was cremated. Everyone was most helpful and thoughtful. The ashes were brought back with Scott's belongings and his car.

We wanted to have a very special and beautiful memorial service for our son; he was a very special and beautiful person. We also wanted his ten-year-old daughter to have something beautiful to remember. At first we weren't sure just how to go ahead, suddenly ideas began coming. I believe Scott must have been helping me; even the poem we used for a memorial card was the first one I looked at.

All our family and friends helped. There was no time to get printing done, nor to order special paper. Our daughter made up a sample memorial card, and we had quick-print copies made on stationery.

The urn, with ashes, was placed in a cut crystal bowl surrounded by red and white rose petals with a tall basket of red and white carnations on each side for the service in the Catholic church. From the church everyone went to the park on the river, where Scott had been best man at his brother's wedding some months before. A service was held there, while Scott's skydiving team flew over the river and scattered the ashes together with a bushel of rose petals. A red or white carnation was given to each of those gathered there to cast upon the water with their special love and a prayer for Scott. Sheri, Scott's daughter, cast a white rose bud.

Since there were a great many people from out of town, we asked everyone to come to our house for refreshments, which had been brought in and were served by our wonderful friends and neighbors. We all shared our memories of Scott; his skydiving awards were presented to us at that time.

IX. Recognition of Death

(Adapted from *The Book of Celebration* by Duke T. Gray and from "A Humanist Funeral Service" by Corliss Lamont and distributed by the Memorial Society of London, Box 4595, London, Ontario N5W 5J5.)

This service may be used either for a funeral service, with the body present, or for a memorial service following burial or cremation. Either service may be done in a church or elsewhere. It is designed to include congregational participation if copies can be made available so that those gathered can take part. This is an important way of helping to evoke the grief and hope which must have its expression. Otherwise, the minister or someone else may simply read the unison or responsive parts.

Music (optional)

Responsive Reading

Reader: Oh, Death, where is your sting?
          Oh, Grave, where is your victory?
Unison: Peace be with us.
Reader: We must all die, and are as water spilt on the ground, which cannot be gathered up again.
Unison: Peace be with us.
Reader: Set me as a seal upon your heart, as a seal upon your arm: for love is strong as death.
Unison: Peace be with us.
Reader: Blessed are those who mourn, for they shall be comforted.
Unison: Peace be with us.
Reader: Blessed are you that weep now, for you shall laugh.
Unison: Peace be with us.
Reader: I have set before you life and death, blessing and cursing: Therefore choose life, that both you and your descendents may live.
Unison: Peace be with us.
Reader: And now abide faith, hope and love, these three; but the greatest of these is love.

The Welcome

Let us call to memory the dead yet ever-living who have passed the doors beyond which we cannot see. They dwell at peace in the halls of memory whose hallowed treasure it is ours to keep, from this day forward.

We have gathered in this place to do honor and praise to the life and memory of _____. We have gathered to offer thanksgiving and gratitude that one such as he/she has lived among us. We have gathered in celebration of death, and in so doing, in celebration of life —for life and death are one, even as the river flows to the sea.

(A candle may be lighted)

Opening Prayer (in unison)

Holy Spirit of Life, and of peace in death, lift our sorrows

Beloved memory and fragile hope, heal the wounds of our mortal loss.

Indestructible remembrance, in whom the spirits of the departed do rest from their labors:

We bless you for the memory of those most dear to us, who have lived in joy and departed in peace.

May we follow the best in them, and, truly loving and serving the gifts they gave us,

Be gathered with them into the life abundant, against whose very richness

The forces of death cannot prevail. Amen.

The Circle of Life

Reader:	To everything there is a season
Unison:	And a time to every purpose under heaven:
Reader:	A time to be born, and a time to die;
Unison:	A time to plant, and a time to harvest;
Reader:	A time to kill, a time to heal;
Unison:	A time to break, and a time to build;
Reader:	A time to weep, and a time to laugh;
Unison:	A time to mourn, and a time to dance
Reader:	A time to cast away stones, and a time to bring stones together;
Unison:	A time to embrace, and a time to be apart;
Reader:	A time to get, and a time to lose;
Unison:	A time to keep silence, a time to speak;
Reader:	We should rejoice in our works, for that is our portion;
Unison:	Cast your bread upon the waters; for you shall find it after many days.

—Ecclesiastes

Music (if desired)

Readings

(Readings, an address or remarks, and/or eulogy or biographical sketch)

"In Memory of W.B. Yeats" (final stanza)   *—W.H. Auden*

"On Death" from *The Prophet*   *—Kahlil Gibran*

Closing Prayer

Now the work is left to us, the living, to carry forth the beauty and joy of that life which has been taken from us. Where we weep, he/she would have us laugh. Where we mourn, he/she would have us rejoice. But we know that he/she will forgive us our grief, for to grieve is to love, to love is to cherish, and to cherish is to give praise and thanksgiving for the life which has blessed us all. To that life we pray courage and strength, that our frailty be forgiven, our sorrows redeemed, the wounds of our loss healed, in the sure knowledge that life moves forward and does not tarry with yesterday, and that the life before us beckons to greater glory as the only memorial that is fitting and just. Amen.

X. Committal Services

A Committal Service for Cremation: Most crematories have an adjacent chapel or an anteroom in which people may gather for a brief ceremony of committal just before the cremation process begins:

> In committing the body of _____ to the flames, we do so with deep reverence for that body as the temple, during life, of a unique and beloved personality. Through the purifying process of fire, this body now becomes transformed into the more simple and ultimate elements of our universe. Fire is, itself, one of the great forces of Nature.
>
> "Fruit-Gathering" by Sir Rabindranath Tagore (See "Selected Readings," pages 139–140,144.)
>
> To the flame, then, we give finally the body of our friend with the full and certain knowledge that, in the words of Socrates, "No evil can befall a good man either in life or after death."

Benediction

> Let us depart in peace, and look to the morning, assured that tomorrow the Sun will rise again.
>
> Life gives, and Life takes away; blessed be life, above all, forever. Amen.

Alternative Benediction

> Now, for us, the living,
>> may the love of friends,
>> the radiance of memory,
>> the fellowship of hope,
>> and the life abundant
>> fill us with all strength and peace,
>> that we may greet the breaking
>> of tomorrow's dawn with praise. Amen.

An Interment Service for Burial: This is a service held at the grave site at the time of burial; sometimes it is called a "graveside."

Opening Words

> Whatsoever things are true,
> Whatsoever things are honest,
> Whatsoever things are just,
> Whatsoever things are pure,
> Whatsoever things are lovely,
> Whatsoever things are of good report:
>> if there be any virtue,
>> and if there be any praise,
> Think on these things.   —Phillipppians 4

> We know in part, and we prophesy in part.
> But when that which is perfect is come,
>> that which is in part shall be done away.
> For now we see through a glass darkly;
>> but then face to face;
> Now I know in part; but then shall I know
>> even as also I am known.   —Corinthians 13

Prayer

Reader: In the midst of life, we are in death.
　　　　　Let us know full well that the spirit of our beloved dwells
　　　　　　　now in our hearts;
　　　　　Let us seek the courage, in love, to carry forward his/her
　　　　　　　memory in the lives we now lead.

Unison: Holy Spirit of Life, receive from us the person of _____.
　　　　　Let the best which was in him/her, be renewed in strength
　　　　　　　in us.
　　　　　May we now give to others the love that we no longer can
　　　　　　　give to him/her,
　　　　　For the lives we lead are now his/her honor and memorial.
　　　　　He/she would bless our sorrows with courage.
　　　　　May our time of pain issue in larger peace.
　　　　　He/she would wish it so;
　　　　　　　　　　So let it be. Amen.

Burial

For as much as the spirit of our brother/sister dwells no more in this mortal form, we commit the body to the ground, earth to earth, ashes to ashes, dust to dust; in the sure knowledge that his/her life continues in us, and that his/her works abide upon the earth. The torch he/she lit, we now carry forward, as also others will pass along ours.
A flower may be tossed into the grave.

> Down gently down
> Softer to sleep
> than bed of night
> From the littleness
> Go.
> Down gently down
> Wider to wake
> Than need of Sun
> Into the greatness
> Go.

XI. A Good-Bye Ceremony for Children

This ceremony was developed in a workshop on celebrations. This workshop tried to create ceremonies for those special situations that are important in our lives, but that are not customarily noted with a ceremony. One group chose to develop an observance to mark the death of a child's pet, but as they talked about, they realized that there are other deaths that might affect a child very deeply — not the devastating loss of a parent or sibling; that would be a different problem altogether. They were thinking of those incomprehensible, bewildering deaths, such as the death of a friend, of a good neighbor, of a slightly known or distant relative, of a teacher.

This ceremony is intended to help a child cope with grief and bewilderment and outrage. It can easily be held at home, but could be held in a schoolroom. It can be conducted by parents (or a parent) for a single child, or for several children. It is important that the expressions be honest — use words like death, sorrow, grief — not euphemisms. It's all right to cry. Begin with a statement of purpose, such as:

"We've gathered together, today, to remember, with love, our friend, Jill, who has died. All living things must die, as we, too, will someday die. It makes us sad that this is so, but no thing lives forever."

Read a poem, or have some music.

Light a candle. "We light this candle; the light will symbolize for us Jill's life, as we think of how much we loved her. Although our sadness is great, we also think how glad we are that she lived, and we are thankful that we knew her, for we had happy times together. If we had some bad times, too, they aren't important now. We loved her; she was a good friend, we'll miss her very much."

Music, or read a poem.

Candlelighting Service: Provide several small candles, and arrange it so that each one can safely be left standing near the large candle — perhaps on a metal tray or in a tray of damp sand. Each child takes a candle, and lighting it at the large candle, says, "I remember ... (something to do with Jill)," then places the small burning candle near the large burning candle.

Extinguish the large candle, saying something like, "Jill, herself, has died, but memories of her, symbolized by these smaller candles, keep on glowing in our hearts and minds, just as the candles keep on glowing." Do not extinguish the candles, let them burn down, or, if the children are going to leave, let them leave while the candles are still burning.

If this is a ceremony for a pet, it could end with burial.

To use flowers instead of candles, have a large bouquet from which each child takes a flower as memories are recalled.

The children should understand, from what you say to them that, although the flowers will fade and die, because nothing living lasts forever, their memories will live on in their minds.

Selected Readings[1]

The following readings are offered for use in planning memorial, funeral, and committal services. They are intended to supplement Biblical and other materials commonly available in reference works for clergy of various faiths.

Wise selection is the key to the effective use of readings. The sensibilities and wishes of the family as they plan the service should be the determining factor.

The readings offer perspective, too, to those contemplating their own death, or reflecting on past bereavement. They can be a source of inspiration and understanding for all students of death education.

General

We meet here in the presence of death to do homage to the Spirit of Life. We would feign make this hour Love's hour and these simple rites Love's confessional. For it is Love's tribute that we come to offer here today.

Our voices may be the voices of grief, but the language after which grief gropes is the language of Love. And we who gather here come in Love's name to express, for those whose lives have been bereft of Love's visible presence, a calm and abiding trust in Love's immortality and consecrating power.   —*Robert Terry Weston*

No one entering this world can ever escape sadness. Each in his turn must bear his burdens, though he be rich or poor, and in his turn bid his loved ones farewell as they set out upon life's ventures. Each one must suffer that sad farewell when loved ones embark on the last voyage, and each in turn must himself take that final journey into the dark.

But to those who make this life a pledge to light and spirit there comes the assurance of a victory that shall redeem life's pain. Though our spirit be but the feeble glow of a candle, there is no dark that it cannot pierce. For him who keeps the candle burning bravely to the end, death is not defeat for light goes on.

—*Robert Terry Weston*

Bitter is the sorrow of bereavement, yet when a loved one passes, remember then the blessing we have received: rejoice that even for so brief a period our life has been enriched and deepened beyond the power of anything to destroy, for never beauty touched the heart of man without creating something eternal.

—*Robert Terry Weston*

And yet I say unto you, be of good courage, for although you may not escape sadness, it is because the life that has departed was rich and sweet that you are sad, and whatever has worth and dignity and beauty is not lost. Nay, this is the testimony not only of the ages since the dawn of time, but this is the message of the test tube and the telescope, even as prophets have proclaimed and poets sung, that nothing is ever lost, but that all things change and move throughout eternity. And dare we not believe that life itself shall be conserved, though bodies die and pass into the earth: yea, and that spirit through the crucible of mortality is not destroyed but purified and enriched and made more great?

—*Robert Terry Weston*

Gitanjali—87

In desperate hope I go and search for her in all the corners of my room; I find her not.

My house is small and what once has gone from it can never be regained.

But infinite is thy mansion, my lord, and seeking her I have come to thy door.

I stand under the golden canopy of thine evening sky and I lift my eager eyes to thy face.

I have come to the brink of eternity from which nothing can vanish—no hope, no happiness, no vision of a face seen through tears.

Oh, dip my emptied life into that ocean, plunge it into the deepest fullness. Let me for once feel that lost sweet touch in the allness of the universe.

—*Rabindranath Tagore*

Gitanjali — 84

It is the pang of separation that spreads throughout the world and gives birth to shapes innumerable in the infinite sky.

It is this sorrow of separation that gazes in silence all night from star to star and becomes lyric among rustling leaves in rainy darkness of July.

It is this overspreading pain that deepens into loves and desires, into sufferings and joys in human homes; and this it is that ever melts and flows in songs through my poet's heart.

—Rabindranath Tagore

Gitanjali — 90

"On the day when death shall knock at thy door, what wilt thou
   offer him?
"Oh, I will set before my guest the full vessel of my life —
   I will never let him go with empty hands.
"All the sweet vintage of my autumn days and summer nights,
   all the earnings and gleanings of my busy life will I place
   before him at the close of my days when death will knock
   at my door."

When I finished she remarked that her vessel was full.

—Rabindranath Tagore

Crossing the Bar

Sunset and evening star,
   And one clear call for me!
And may there be no moaning of the bar,
   When I put out to sea,

But such a tide as moving seems asleep,
   Too full for sound and foam,
When that which drew from out the boundless deep
   Turns again home.

Twilight and evening bell,
   And after that the dark!
And may there be no sadness of farewell,
   When I embark;

For though from out our bourne of Time and Place
   The flood may bear me far,
I hope to see my Pilot face to face
   When I have crossed the bar.

—Alfred, Lord Tennyson

Fruit-Gathering: XLVI

The time is past when I could repay
her for all that I received.

Her night has found its morning and
thou hast taken her to thy arms: and to
thee I bring my gratitude and my gifts
that were for her.

For all hurts and offences to her I
come to thee for forgiveness.

I offer to thy service those flowers of
my love that remained in bud when she
waited for them to open.

—Rabindranath Tagore

Fruit-Gathering: XLIX

The pain was great when the strings
were being tuned, my Master!

Begin your music, and let me forget
the pain; let me feel in beauty what you
had in your mind through those pitiless
days.

The waning night lingers at my
doors, let her take her leave in songs.

Pour your heart into my life strings,
my Master, in tunes that descend from
your stars.

—Rabindranath Tagore

In Memoriam: LIII

O yet we trust that somehow good
    Will be the final goal of ill,
    To pangs of nature, sins of will,
Defects of doubt, and taints of blood;

That nothing walks with aimless feet;
    That not one life shall be destroy'd,
    Or cast as rubbish to the void,
When God hath made the pile complete;

That not a worm is cloven in vain;
    That not a moth with vain desire
    Is shrivel'd in a fruitless fire,
Or but subserves another's gain.

Behold, we know not anything;
    I can but trust that good shall fall
    At last—far off—at last, to all.
And every winter change to spring.

So runs my dream: but what am I?
    An infant crying in the night:
    An infant crying for the light:
And with no language but a cry.

—Alfred, Lord Tennyson

O God, eternal spirit of love and righteousness, through whose
constant presence in our hearts we are made strong, and by whom we
live, we come unto thee in this time of sorrow, and we are sustained
by thine indwelling presence.

Thou teachest us to be reconciled unto sorrow; thou turnest
sorrow into a universal sympathy and compassion. Trusting in thee we
learn not merely to endure but to rejoice in life as a far more eternal
and abiding thing than human flesh.

Not for ourselves along, but for all who suffer and are afflicted by grief, we pray, that consciousness of thine eternity of fulfillment may uplift and sustain, and thy compassion minister to them through human hands.

May we learn to be glad for that which has been, not as something taken away but as something given to us even if for a brief time, through which we have been blessed. Teach us, we pray, to rejoice again, to share all beauty we have known, all love, all hope, all faith, and to be grateful for they tender hand which at the end bringeth release in peace and blessed sleep.

—Robert Terry Weston

I had rather think of those I have loved and lost as having returned to earth, as having become a part of the elemental wealth of the world, I would rather dream of them as unconscious dust; I would rather dream of them as laughing in the stream, floating in the clouds, bursting in light upon the shores of other worlds; I would rather think of them as the lost visions of a forgotten night, than to have even the faintest fear ... But as for me, I will leave the dead where nature leaves them. Whatever flower of hope springs in my heart I will cherish; I will give it breath of sighs and rain of tears.

—R.G. Ingersoll, "The House of Death"

O thou, who art the inspirer of the faith that burns ever more brightly within the souls of men, unto thee do we turn in this time of testing. Within us do well up the great mysteries of the ages. The unanswered questions of all saddened hearts are on our lips. We would be assured and comforted if that might be within the power of our hearts to know and understand. But as we pause to honor a memory made beautiful by life, we pray only that our faith be strengthened by the faith that was so strong in him.

Maker of Mysteries, guide thou us whose spiritual vision is dim and uncertain. As the joy of close comradeship is withdrawn, do thou come with thy divine fellowship and renew our confidence in the everlasting life of the spirit of man.

—Francis G. Ricker

Mourn Not the Dead

Mourn not the dead that in the cool earth lie
Dust unto dust—
The calm, sweet earth that mothers all who die
As all men must;

But rather mourn the apathetic throng—
The cowed and meek
Who see the world's great anguish and its wrong
And dare not speak!

—Ralph Chaplin

A Scriptural Message for Use in a Memorial Service
by *Rev. Philip Nordstrom* (adapted):

God is our refuge and strength, our constant help in every sorrow;
Therefore we will not fear even though this earthly dust be removed
and be carried into the Eternal Sea,

For therein is a river whose fountains gladden the City of God, the holy temples of his dwelling place.
Come behold now this work of the Lord, what transformations he hath wrought on this earth, in this holy clay:
He hath made an end to this transitory struggle,
He hath unbent this bow, and shattered the shaft,
And he hath refined as in fire, this mortal chariot unto immortality.[1]

Comfort ye, comfort ye, my people, saith your God.
Speak ye comfortably to Jerusalem and say unto her that her iniquity is pardoned.
For he shall lead his flock like a shepherd,
He shall carry the lambs in his arms and gently lead those that are with young.

Have you not known?
Have you not heard that the everlasting God, the creator of the ends of the earth fainteth not, neither is weary.
For he giveth power to the faint and to them that have no might He increaseth strength.
They shall walk and not faint, they shall run and not be weary, they shall mount up with wings as eagles.[2]

Behold, I will not leave you comfortless, but I will come unto you, and I will make my abode with you, and will come in and sup with you.[3]
In this world, ye shall have tribulation but be of good cheer, I have overcome the world.[4]
My peace I give unto you; not as the world gives, give I unto you.[5]
Behold! I will give you the oil of gladness instead of mourning, and sorrowing and sighing shall be done away.[6]

Come unto Me, all ye that labor and are heavy laden and I will give you rest.
Take my yoke upon you and learn of me, for I am meek and lowly in heart, for my yoke is easy and my burden is light.[7]
Incline your ear, and come unto me, hear, and your soul shall live.[8]
Remember that the eternal God is thy refuge and underneath are the everlasting arms.

Comfort ye! Comfort ye, my people!
Says your God.

For a Child

We are hurting, Lord. With our child's death went all our hopes, our dreams, our future.

But in our grief we can now fully appreciate the little things in life. We are thankful for even the short time we had with our child. We realize how fragile and brief life can be. We now take nothing for granted.

---

[1]Based on Psalm 46. [2]Isaiah 40:1–2, 11, 28–31. [3]John 14:18,23. [4]John 16:33. [5]John 14:27. [6]Isaiah 61:3. [7]Matthew 11:28-30. [8]Isaiah 56:3.

Thank you for being with us in our time of sadness and grief. We look to you for strength.

—From burial service for Benjamin Matthew Jones

In the flesh there is no continuing life, for things that are of flesh must perish after the way of flesh; yet there is no spirit however weak or faint, however young, but leaves its glow upon the world; no spirit, however long or short its sojourn here, but speaks of greater and enduring life through its own sublime mystery and beauty. The spirit is of the nature of eternity: even as it smiles upon us here, suddenly there is a light about our heads and life is changed. So this bright spark of the eternal fire is not lost in death. The first brave smile of the tiniest babe kindles a warmth in other hearts that shall never die. Though death strike sorrow to our hearts, the glory of that smile still lingers within, to outlive sorrow and bind us to all childhood with enfolding love.

—Robert Terry Weston

For the Aged

Beautiful are the youth whose rich emotions flash and burn, whose lithe bodies filled with energy and grace sway in their happy dance of life; and beautiful likewise are the mature who have learned compassion and patience, charity and wisdom, though they be rarer far than beautiful youth. But most beautiful and most rare is a gracious old age which has drawn from life the skill to take its varied strands: the harsh advance of age, the pang of grief, the passing of dear friends, the loss of strength, and with fresh insight weave them into a rich and gracious pattern all its own. This is the greatest skill of all, to take the bitter with the sweet and make it beautiful, to take the whole of life in all its moods, its strengths and weaknesses, and of the whole make one great and celestial harmony.

—Robert Terry Weston

For a Parent

Blessed are they who rear their families in honor and in gentleness, who live courageous and upright lives, who live life in its fullness, do their part, and then at eventide retire to rest.

Though pain be in the heart, let none grieve, for here a gentle soul has cast its glow upon us, and like the glory of an autumn sun, has lit the world with kindness through its day, and at the close has gently sunk to rest.

Rather rejoice for that which (she) has given, the light we know and treasure still within our hearts, a light we trust still shineth beyond the distant peaks (this world's horizon), for life goes on, and spirit knows no death.

—Robert Terry Weston

For Burial Committal Services

Requiem

Fall softly, O thou coat of winter snow, and keep our loved one warm;
Kiss him gently, sun and rain, in the quiet of his rest;
Watch over him, wind and stars, in the silence of the night;

Grow thou to cover him, grass and flowers, and make beautiful his
    couch,
And thou, Great Spirit of Love and Peace, take him into thine arms
    and lull him to rest forevermore. Amen.

—*Rev. John G. MacKinnon*

Deep wet moss and cool blue shadows
    Beneath a bending fir,
And the purple solitude of mountains,
    When only the dark owls stir—
Oh, there will come a day, a twilight,
    When I shall sink to rest
In deep wet moss and cool blue shadows
    Upon a mountain's breast,
And yield a body torn with passions,
    And bruised with earthly scars,
To the cool oblivion of evening,
    Of solitude and stars.

—*Lew Sarett*

Song

She's somewhere in the sunlight strong,
Her tears are in the falling rain,
She calls me in the wind's soft song.
And with the flowers she comes again.

Yon bird is but her messenger,
The moon is but her silver car;
Yea! sun and moon are sent by her,
And every wistful waiting star.

—*Richard LeGallienne*

For Cremation Committal Service

Fruit-Gathering:XL

O Fire, my brother, I sing victory to you.

You are the bright red image of fearful freedom.

You swing your arms in the sky, you sweep your impetuous
fingers across the harp-string, your dance music is beautiful.

When my days are ended and the gates are opened you will
burn to ashes this cordage of hands and feet.

My body will be one with you, my heart will be caught in
the whirls of your frenzy, and the burning heat that was my
life will flash up and mingle itself in your flame.

—*Rabindranath Tagore*

It is but fitting that we should commit this body to the flame
So like that which but recently did burn
Within that fine brave head.
It is as if he doth return
Unto the fountain whence he came,
Source of all spirits bright,
The comradeship and life of all pure souls,
As now he enters into purifying light.

—*Robert Terry Weston*

Additional Readings

"To W.P.II." by George Santayana
"Dirge Without Music," by Edna St. Vincent Millay
"Death," "Joy and Sorrow," and "Pain," from *The Prophet* by Kahlil Gibran.
Psalms 19, 23 and 121.

REFERENCE

[1]Quotations by Robert Terry Weston, R.G. Ingersoll, Francis G. Ricker, Rev. John G. MacKinnon, and Richard LeGallienne, are taken from *A Cup of Strength: Readings in Time of Sorrow and Bereavement*, compiled by Robert Terry Weston, 1945. Reprinted by permission from Robert Terry Weston.

Information and Coordination

The American Association of Tissue Banks. 1350 Beverly Rd., Suite 220-A, McLean, VA 22101, (703) 827-9582. Nongovernmental group of physicians, nurses, lawyers, technicians and the general public. Develops standards for tissue banking. Inspects and certifies tissue banks. Certifies personnel.

Eye Bank Association of America. 1725 Eye St. N.W., Suite 308, Washington DC 20006-2403, (202) 775-4999. Develops standards, professional training, and computer coordination; and monitors government activity and the media.

Eye Bank of Canada. The Canadian Institute for the Blind, 1929 Fairview Avenue, Toronoto, Ontario M4G 3E8. Clearing house for Canadian eye banks.

The Living Bank. P.O. Box 6725, Houston, TX 77265 (800) 528-2971. See Chapter 8, "How the Dead Can Help the Living," p.00

Medic Alert. Turlock, CA 95381-1009, (209) 668-3333. (See Chapter 8, "How the Dead Can Help the Living." p.00.)

Organ Donors Canada. 5326 Ada Boulevard, Edmonton, Alberta T5W 4N7, (403) 474-9363. Founded in 1974, this is a nonprofit lay organization devoted to increasing public awareness of the need for organ and tissue donation.

Transplant International. 339 Windermere Rd., London, Ont. N6A 5A5, (519) 663-3709. Publishes free quarterly transplant newsletter called "Transplant Lifelines."

United Network for Organ Sharing(UNOS). P.O. Box 13770, Richmond, VA 23225, (804) 330-8500. Founded in 1984, a nationwide, computerized network for matching transplant donations and recipients through its membership of 251 transplant centers, 52 independent organ procurement agencies, and 39 tissue typing laboratories. In October 1986 received the federal contracts to operate the national Organ Procurement and Transplantation Network (OPTN) and the National Scientific Registry.

Uniform Donor Cards

Uniform donor cards may be obtained from The Living Bank, Medic Alert, and Organ Donors Canada, addresses above; and from the Continental Association of Funeral and Memorial Societies, see Appendix 6, "Directory of Memorial Societies," and Kidney Foundations, addresses on page 149 of this appendix. (See illustration on page 156.)

Canadian Regional Organ Procurement and Exchange Programs

ALBERTA: *Calgary:* Human Organ Procurement & Exchange Program, Foothills Provincial General Hosp., 1403 29th St., NW, T2N 2T9, (403) 283-2243.

Edmonton: Human Organ Procurement & Exchange Program, University of Alberta Hospitals, 8440 112 St., T6G 2B7, (403) 492-1970

BRITISH COLUMBIA: *Vancouver:* Pacific Organ Retrieval for Transplantation, Vancouver Gen. Hosp., 855 - 12th Ave., V5Z 1M9, (604) 875-4665.

MANITOBA: *Winnipeg:* Manitoba Transplant Program, Health Sciences Centre, 700 William Ave., R3E 0Z3, (204) 787-2071, Ext.505.

NEW BRUNSWICK: *Saint John:* Organ Procurement for Transplantation, Saint John Regional Hosp., E2L 4L2, (506) 648-6848

NEWFOUNDLAND: *St. John's:* Organ Procurement & Exchange Program, Health Sciences Complex, A1B 3V6, (709) 737-6600.

NOVA SCOTIA: *Halifax:* Multi-Organ Transplant Program, Victoria Gen. Hosp., B3H 2Y9, (902) 428-5504.

ONTARIO: *Toronto:* Multiple Organ Retrieval and Exchange Program, 200 Elizabeth St., M5C 2G4, (800) 387-MORE, (416) 595-3587.

QUEBEC: *Montreal:* Metro Transplantation, 1560 Sherbrooke St., E., H2L 4K8, (514) 876-6768.

SASKATCHEWAN: *Saskatoon:* Renal Transplant Program, Univ. Hosp., S7N 0X0, (306) 966-7985.

Related Legislation

The National Organ Transplant Act was passed by the United States Congress in 1984. It provided for a Task Force to study the "medical, legal, ethical, economic, and social issues presented by human organ procurement and transplantation." The Act authorizes the funding of the contracted Organ Procurement and Transplantation Network as a clearinghouse for transplant centers, and prohibits the purchase of organs.

In 1982, the U.S. Conference of Commissioners on Uniform State Laws recommended a Uniform Determination of Death Act and most states now have effective this Act or an equivalent. This defines death as the irreversible cessation of all brain and brain stem function, thus allowing artificial maintenance of heartbeat and respiration to preserve needed organs without raising doubt that the person is in fact dead.

In Canada, all provinces have now adopted some form of the Model Human Tissues Gift Act recommended by the Conference of Commissioners on Uniformity of Legislation in Canada in 1970.

Specific Anatomical Gifts[1]

Eyes.   The most frequently transplanted of all human tissues (except bone tissues) are the corneas, or lenses of eyes. Thousands of blind people have had their sight restored in this way. In 1988 there were 2,236 corneas transplanted in Canada. In the United States 42,104 corneas were used for transplant and other surgical procedures. Not all vision defects can be cured by transplants, and it is not possible to transplant the whole eye, but sight can be restored by corneal transplant in most cases of common corneal diseases. In North America there are thousands of blind people whose sight could be restored if enough corneas were available. In 1988 37,000 eyes were used for training and research.

Always carry a Uniform Donor Card and be sure to check the Eye Bank square. Call your nearest eye bank for instructions on how to assure that your gift is used, and for more information on how eye donations are used in your area. (See Directory on pp. 00.) It does not matter if you wear glasses or what your age, race or blood type may be. Eyes must be removed by trained personnel within a few hours of death. This can be done in the hospital or at home. Some funeral directors are trained to do this. Eyes may not be bequeathed to specific individuals, but must be used on a first-come first-served basis regardless of ability to pay. Airlines transport them without charge. Unlike other organs, the donation of eyes does not prevent leaving one's body to a medical school. Likewise, it makes no difference in the appearance of the body for viewing.

Kidneys.   First and most frequent of major organs to be transplanted, 9,123 kidneys were transplanted in the U.S. in 1988, 702 in Canada in 1989. Patient survival rates after one year are now as high as ninety-seven percent for kidneys from related donors and ninety percent with cadaver organs. In 1985 in the U.S. nearly 85,000 patients were kept alive by artificial kidney machines (dialysis), of whom 10,000 were waiting for a kidney transplant. In March 1990, 16,930 patients were waiting for kidney transplants in the U.S. Thousands more donated kidneys are needed than are available each year. For further information, contact the National Kidney Foundation, 2 Park Avenue, New York, NY 10016, (212)889-2210, or the Kidney Foundation of Canada, Suite 555, 4060 St. Catherine Street West, Montreal, Que. H3Z 2Z3, 1- (800) 361-7994. Consult local telephone directories or national offices for addresses of local branches.

Blood.   This is the most commonly "transplanted" tissue, with three to four million transfusions occurring annually in the U.S. alone. There has been some experimentation with the use of cadaver blood, which has some advantages, but this is not as yet being practiced because of prohibitive costs Improved technology may remedy that. There is still a great need for volunteer donation of blood. The shortage of volunteer blood has led to the widespread use of commercial blood, with a resultant high rate of post-transfusion complications. Volunteers have no reason to conceal their health records; paid donors do. Although blood is tested for hepatitis and AIDS, the tests are not one hundred percent reliable. It is estimated that ten percent of recipients of transfusions eventually develop hepatitis, and that about fifty recipients each year will develop AIDS. For this reason, it is becoming common practice when possible to store a patient's own blood for subsequent use during surgery. For further information, contact the Blood Services Laboratories, American Red Cross, 15601 Crabbs Branch Way, Rockville, MD 20855, or Blood Transfusion Service, The Canadian Red Cross Society, 1800 Alta Vista Drive, Ottawa, Ontario, K1G 4J5.

Ear Tissues.   Persons over the age of five years (no upper age limit), even those with nerve related hearing impairments, can bequeath their middle ear tissue to restore hearing to as many as six individuals with conductive hearing loss. Cause of death must be provided with donation. The Ear Bank of Project HEAR has provided over 25,000 ear implants since 1969. For further information, contact Project HEAR, 801 Welch Rd., Palo Alto, CA 94304, (415) 494-2000. In Canada the Ontario Temporal Bone Bank is gone but there is now the Ear Bank of British Columbia, 865 W. 10th Ave., Vancouver, BC V5Z 1L7, (604) 876-3211. Local 3212. Conducts research and supplies temporal bones and tympanic membranes for transplant. Solicits tissues from both normal and impaired. Requests medical histories.

Ear Tissues for Research.   As above, persons with hearing problems or ear disorders are urged to bequeath ear structures for research, along with a medical history from the donor's doctor. Removal of ear structures (a specialized task) is arranged in the U.S. by the National Temporal Bone Banks Center of the Deafness Research Foundation, 9 E. 38th St., New York, NY 10016.

Livers.   There were 1,680 livers transplanted in the U.S. in 1988, while there were 121 liver transplants in Canada.

Hearts.   In 1988, there were 1,647 heart transplants in the U.S., and 185 in Canada.

Single Lung, Double Lung, and Heart/Lung.   In 1988, there were 74 heart/lung transplants in the U.S. and 31 lung transplants. In Canada there were 6 heart/lung and 16 lung transplants.

Brain Tissue.   Post mortem research into Alzheimer's disease, Parkinson's disease, epilepsy, multiple sclerosis and other disorders involving brain pathology is being conducted with donated brain and other nerve tissue. Normal brain tissue is also urgently needed for this research. Contact the Canadian Brain Tissue Bank, Room 127, Banting Institute, 100 College Street, Toronto, Ontario M5G 1L5, (416) 977-3398, or the Brain Tissue Resource Center, Ralph Lowell Laboratories, Harvard Medical School, 115 Mill St., Belmont, MA 02178, (617) 855-2400.

Pancreases.   In 1988, 243 pancreases were transplanted in the U.S. and 2 in Canada.

Other Organs.   Many other tissues are valuable in promoting health and saving lives — among them cartilage, iliac crests, dura mater, fascia lata, joints and bone marrow.

Artificial Implants.   Post mortem donation of devices such as pacemakers, bone wire and screws, joints and other artificial implants, with permission to analyze related tissues, can be extremely helpful for research on how such implants perform and interact with human tissue once in place.

Eyeglasses.   In the U.S., eyeglasses may be donated to New Eyes for the Needy, Box 332, 549 Millburn Ave., Short Hills, NJ 07078, (201) 376-4093, which receives and distributes them through medical missions and hospitals overseas. Sale of donated jewelry and precious metal scrap (gold dental crowns, eyeglass frames, earrings, etc.) fund new eyeglasses for U.S. recipients. In Canada, eyeglasses may be sent to Operation Eyesight Universal, 4 Parkdale Cr. NW, Calgary, Alta. T2N 3T8, (403) 283-6323.

Canadian Eye Bank Coordinators

ALBERTA: *Calgary:* Susan Sim, Technical Director, Lions Eye Bank of Alberta, c/o Rockyview General Hospital, 7007 14th St. S.W., T2V 1P9 (403) 259-7660.

    Edmonton: Mae Cox, Coordinator, Lions Eye Bank, 12010 Jasper Ave., T5K 0P3 (403) 482-4988

BRITISH COLUMBIA: *Vancouver:* Mark Soper, Transplant Coordinator, Eye Bank of British Columbia, University of British Columbia / Vancouver General Hospital Eye Care Centre, 2550 Willow Street V5Z 3N9 (604) 875-4567

MANITOBA: *Winnipeg:* Carol Gerrie, Coordinator, Lions Eye Bank of Manitoba & Northwestern Ontario, Inc., 700 William Ave. R3E 0Z8 (204) 787-3443

ONTARIO: *Toronto:* Anne Wolf, Executive Secretary, Eye Bank of Canada (Ontario), 1 Spadina Crescent M5S 2J5 (CNIB)(416) 978-2637/-486-2520

QUEBEC: *Montreal:* Monique Slovic, Executive Secretary, Foundation de la

Banque d'Yeux du Quebec, Inc., 5689 Boul. Rosemont H1T 2H1 (514) 252-3886.

Ste. Foy: Celine Lemey, Banque d'Yeux Nationale Inc., 2705 Boul. Laurier G1V 4G2 (418) 654-2702.

SASKATCHEWAN: *Saskatoon:* Ruth Pollack, Lions Eye Bank of Saskatchewan Inc., c/o Eye Depart., University Hospital S7N 0X0 (306) 966-1002.

In the eastern provinces, donations are handled by the multi-organ donor programs.

Eye Banks of U.S. *(Members of the Eye Bank Assn. of America)*

ALABAMA: *Birmingham:* Alabama Eye and Tissue Bank, 700 South 18th St., 35233 (205) 939-3937

Huntsville: Alabama Eye and Tissue Bank, North Regional Office, 120 Governors Drive, Suite 110 35801 (205) 534-3937

Mobile: Alabama Eye and Tissue Bank, Southwest Regional Office, 2451 Fillingim Street 36617 (205) 476-3937

Montgomery: Alabama Eye and Tissue Bank, Central Regional Office, 2125 East South Blvd. 36199 (205) 288-3937

Sheffield: Lion Eye and Temporal Bone Bank, Helen Keller Memorial Hospital, PO Box 610, 1300 S. Montgomery Avenue 35660 (205) 386-4202

ARIZONA: *Phoenix:* Arizona Lions Eye Bank, St. Luke's Medical Center, 1800 East Van Buren 85006 (800) 776-2585 (24 hours)

Tucson: Arizona Lions Eye Bank, St. Joseph's Hospital, 350 North Wilmot 85710 (602) 296-3211 (24 hours)

ARKANSAS: *Little Rock:* Arkansas Eye & Kidney Bank, 4301 West Markham (U.A.M.S. Slot 577) 72206 (501) 664-4990

Little Rock: The Arkansas Eye Bank & Laboratory, Univ. or Arkansas for Medical Sciences, 4301 West Markham, Slot 523 72210 (501) 666-3937

CALIFORNIA: *Fresno:* Lions Eye Bank of the San Joaquin Valley, Inc., 1360 E. Herndon Avenue, Suite 230 93710 (209) 449-2020

Loma Linda: Loma Linda Eye and Tissue Bank-TBI, 1130 Anderson St., P.O. Box 1710 92354 (714) 824-4501

Los Angeles: Lions Doheny Eye Bank-TBI, 1355 San Pablo St. 90033 (213) 223-0333

Los Angeles: UCLA Eye Bank, Jules Stein Eye Institute, UCLA School of Medicine 90024 (213) 825-6095

Orange: Lions-UCI Eye Bank 101 The City Drive, Route 162 92668-3297 (714) 634-6965

Sacramento: Lions Eye & Tissue Bank, Department of Ophthalmology, University of California, 2315 Stockton Blvd., Trailer 1527 95817 (916) 453-2298

San Diego: San Diego Eye Bank-TBI, 4077 Fifth Ave. 92103 (619) 294-8267

San Francisco: Lions Eye Bank of Northern California, Transplant Bank at Pacific Medical Center, P.O. Box 7999 94120 (415) 922-3100

Santa Ana: Orange County Eye and Tissue Bank-TBI, 640 N. Tustin Ave., Suite 101 92705 (714) 550-1022

COLORADO: *Colorado Springs:*Rocky Mountain Lions Eye Bank, 12 N. Meade Ave. 80909 (719) 630-1001

Denver: Colorado Eye Bank, 3500 East 12th Avenue 80206 (303) 399-6519

Denver: Rocky Mountain Lions Eye Bank, Colorado Expo-Plaza, 695 S. Colorado Blvd. Ste. 320 80222 (303) 778-0282

CONNECTICUT: *New Britain:* Connecticut Eye Bank, New Britain General Hospital, 100 Grand Street 06052 (203) 224-5550

DELAWARE: *Wilmington:* Medical Eye Bank of Delaware, 501 W. 14th St. 19899 (302) 656-5078 (24 hours)

DISTRICT OF COLUMBIA: *Washington:* Washington Eye Bank-TBI, 3800 Reservoir Rd. N.W., Suite 518 20007 (202) 737-6753

Seabrook, Md.: Lions Eye Bank, 9470 Annapolis Road, Suite 417 20706 (301) 577-7800/(202) 393-2265 (24 hours)

FLORIDA: *Ft. Myers:* Lifelink of SW Florida, 1500-F Matthew Dr. 33907 (813) 936-2772

Orlando: Medical Eye Bank of Florida-TBI, 1220 Lucerne Terrace 32806 (407) 422-2020

Tampa: Central Florida Lions Eye Bank, Inc., 13331 Magnolia Drive 33612 (813) 977-1300

GEORGIA: *Atlanta:* Georgia Lions Eye Bank, Inc., Emory University, 1327 Clifton Road, N.E. 30322 (404) 321-9300

Augusta: Medical College of Georgia Eye Bank, Department of Ophthalmology 30912 (404) 724-1388

HAWAII: *Honolulu:* Hawaii Lions Eye Bank & Makana Foundation, P.O. Box 2783, 888 South King Street 96803 (808) 536-7416

IDAHO: *Boise:* Idaho Lions Eye Bank, St. Alphonsus Regional Medical Center, 1055 North Curtis Road 83706 (208) 378-2400 (nights and weekends)

ILLINOIS: *Chicago:* Illinois Eye Bank-MEBTC, 800 South Wells 60607 (312) 996-9467

Normal: Mennonite Hospital-Watson Gailey Eye Foundation Eye Bank, Brokaw Hospital, Virginia at Franklyn 61761 (309) 454-1400

INDIANA: *Indianapolis:* Indiana Lions Eye Bank, Inc., Department of Ophthalmology, Indiana University Medical Center, 702 Rotary Circle 46202-2684 (317) 274-8527 (Day) 274-5000 (Night resident on call)

Indianapolis: Midwest Eye Institute Eye Bank, Methodist Hospital of Indiana, 1701 N. Senate Blvd., P.O. Box 1367 46206 (317) 926-2333.

IOWA: *Iowa City:* Iowa Lions Eye Bank, Department of Ophthalmology, University of Iowa Hospitals & Clinics 52242 (319) 356-2215/1616

KANSAS: *Kansas City:* Kansas Eye Bank, Department of Ophthalmology, University of Kansas, Medical Center, 39th & Rainbow 66103 (913) 588-6658

Wichita: Wichita Eye Bank, 3306 E. Central 67208 (316) 688-3937.

KENTUCKY: *Lexington:* University of Kentucky Lions Eye Bank, University of Kentucky Medical Center, 800 Rose Street 40356-0084 (606) 233-6740

Louisville: Univ. of Louisville Lions Eye Bank, 301 E. Muhammad Ali Blvd. 40202 (502) 588-5466/(800) 525-3456

LOUISIANA: *Baton Rouge:* Our Lady of the Lake Regional Medical Center, 5000 Hennessy Blvd. 70808 (504) 769-3100/766-8996 (24 hours)

New Orleans: Southern Eye Bank, 4440 Magnolia St. 70115 (504) 891-3937

Shreveport: Northwest Louisiana Lions Eye Bank, 1508 W. Kirby Place, Suite 100 71103 (318) 622-7999

MARYLAND: *Baltimore:* Tissue Banks International, (Headquarters of TBI), also: the Medical Eye Bank of Maryland-TBI, 815 Park Avenue 21201 (301) 752-3800

MASSACHUSETTS: *Boston:* New England Eye Bank-TBI, 100 Charles River Plaza Cambridge St., 6th Floor 02114 (617) 523-3937

MICHIGAN: *Ann Arbor:* Michigan Eye Bank & Transplantation Center, (MEBT Headquarters), 1000 Wall Street, Kellogg Eye Center 48105-1994 (313) 764-5106

Detroit: Wayne State University Division-MEBTC, 4160 John R., Suite 503 48201 (313) 677-1329

Marquette: Upper Peninsula Division of the Michigan Eye Bank-MEBTC, Marquette General Hospital, 420 West Magnet St. 49855 (906) 225-3580

MINNESOTA: *Minneapolis:* Minnesota Lions Eye Bank, Department of Ophthalmology, 9-240 Health Sciences, Unit C, 516 Delaware Street, S.E. 55455 (612) 624-0433 (Office — day)/624-3900 (Lab — day)/626-3062(Emergency hours)

Rochester: Mayo Clinic Eye Bank, 200 S.W. First Street 55905 (507) 284-3760

MISSISSIPPI:*Jackson:* Mississippi Lions Eye Bank, Inc., 5455 Executive Place 39206 (601) 984-5030 (24 hours)

MISSOURI: *Columbia:* Missouri Lions Eye Tissue Bank, 404 Portland 65201 (314) 443-1479 (24 hours)

Kansas City: Kansas City Eye Bank-TBI, 2727 Main, Suite 110 64108 (816) 472-7177

St. Louis: American Red Cross Bistate Chapter Tissue Bank, 4050 Lindell Blvd. 63108 (314) 658-2193

St. Louis: St. Louis Eye Bank, 660 South Euclid 63110 (314) 362-2020 (Day)/362-4075 (Night)

MONTANA: *Missoula:* Montana Eye Bank Foundation, 554 W. Broadway, 59806 (406) 728-2115

NEBRASKA: *Omaha:* Lions Eye Bank of Nebraska, University of Nebraska Medical Center, 42nd & Dewey Avenue 68105 (402) 559-4039 (24 hours)

NEVADA: *Las Vegas:* Nevada Eye Bank, 620 Shadow Lane 89106 (702) 386-3937

NEW JERSEY: *Newark:* Lions Eye Bank of New Jersey, Eye Institute of New Jersey, 15 South 9th Street 07107 (201) 456-4626 (24 hours)

NEW MEXICO:*Albuquerque:* New Mexico Lions Eye Bank, Presbyterian Professional Building, 201 Cedar, S.E., Suite B-1 87106 (505) 841-1210 (24 hours)

NEW YORK:*Albany:* Sight Conservation Society of Northeastern New York, Inc., Hun Bldg., Albany Medical College, New Scotland Avenue, 12208 (518) 445-5199

Buffalo: Buffalo Eye Bank & Research Society, Inc., 2550 Main Street 14214 (716) 832-5448 (Day)/835-8725 (Night)

Manhasset: Lions Eye Bank for Long Island, North Shore Univ. Hospital 11030 (516) 562-1069

New York: Eye-Bank for Sight Restoration, Inc., 210 East 64th Street 10021 (212) 980-6700/838-9211 (Corneal Lab — 24 hours)

Rochester: Rochester Eye & Human Parts Bank, 224 Alexander Street 14607 (716) 546-5250 (24 hours)/275-2508 (Lab)

Syracuse: Central New York Eye Bank & Research Corporation, SUNY Health Sciences Center, 750 E. Adamst St. 13201 (315) 471-6060 (24 hour answering service)

NORTH CAROLINA: *Asheville:* N.C. Eye & Human Tissue Bank, Inc., Western Branch, St. Joseph's Hospital, 428 Biltmore Ave. 28801 (704) 258-3218

Charlotte: N.C. Eye & Human Tissue Bank, Inc., Charlotte Memorial Hospital & Medical Ctr., P.O. Box 32861 28232 (704) 338-2000

Durham: N.C. Eye & Human Tissue Bank, Inc., Westgate Plaza, 3622 Lyckan Parkway, Suite 6002 27707 (919) 489-8404

Greenville: N.C. Eye & Human Tissue Bank, Inc., Carolina Organ Procurement Agency, 702 Johns Hopkins Drive 27834 (919) 757-0090

Winston-Salem: North Carolina Eye & Human Tissue Bank, Inc. (Headquarters), 3195 Maplewood Avenue 27103 (919) 765-0932

OHIO: *Canton:* Melvin E. Jones Eye Bank, 1320 Timken Mercy Drive 44708 (216) 489-1174/(800) 325-4444

Cincinnati: Cincinnati Eye Bank, College of Medicine, University of Cincinnati Medical Center, 231 Bethesda Avenue, Room 6001-A 45267-0527 (513) 861-3716

Cleveland: Cleveland Eye Bank, 1909 East 101st St. Suite 10 44106 (216) 791-9700

Columbus: Central Ohio Lions Eye Bank, Inc., 456 West 10th Ave., UHC 43210 (614) 293-8114

Dayton: Lions eye Bank of W. Central Ohio-TBI, 40 South Perry St., Suite 140 45402

Toledo: Eye Bank of Northwestern Ohio, Medical College of Ohio, P.O. Box 10008 43699 (419) 381-4172

OKLAHOMA: *Oklahoma City:* Oklahoma Lions Eye Bank, 711 Stanton L. Young Blvd., Suite 100 73104 (405) 271-5691

Tulsa: Oklahoma Lions Eye Bank, 1923 S. Utica Ave. 74104 (918) 749-3937

OREGON: *Medford:* Lions Eyebank of Oregon, Southern Region Laboratory, 228 Holly St. 97501 (503) 779-4958

Portland: Lions Eye Bank of Oregon, 1010 N.W. 22nd Avenue, N120 97210-3026 (503) 229-7523

Portland: Oregon Eye Bank, 3181 SW Sam Jackson Pike Rd. LA67 97201 (503) 279-8690

PENNSYLVANIA: *Erie:* Greater Erie Eye Bank, Inc., 2402 Cherry Street 16502-2693 (814) 459-3545

Hershey: Lions Eye Bank of Central Pennsylvania, P.O. Box 850 17033 (717) 531-6053

Philadelphia: Lions Eye Bank of Delaware Valley, Wills Eye Hospital, 9th & Walnut Streets 19107 (215) 627-0700/-(800) 462-1011 (Toll Free, PA residents)/(800) 523-1011 (Toll Free, CT, NY, MD, DE & NJ residents)

Pittsburg: Medical Eye Bank of Western Pennsylvania, 203 Lothrop St. 15213 (412) 647-8500

PUERTO RICO: *San Juan:* Lions Eye Bank of Puerto Rico, P.O. Box 3311, 3311 General Post Office 00936-3311 (809) 783-8800

SOUTH CAROLINA: *Charleston:* South Carolina Lions Eye Bank, Inc.-MUSC, Storm Eye Institute, 171 Ashley Ave. 29425 (803)792-9296

West Columbia: South Carolina Lions Eye Bank, Inc., 110 Lexington Medical Mall 29169 (803) 796-1304

SOUTH DAKOTA: *Sioux Falls:* Lions (Mid-Central) Eye Bank of South Dakota, 1701 S. Minnesota Avenue 57105 (605) 334-7715

TENNESSEE: *Chattanooga:* District 12-0 Lions Eye bank and Sight Service, 975 E. 3rd Street, P.O. Box 100 37403 (615) 778-4000

Knoxville: East Tennessee Eye Bank, 1924 Alcoa Highway, U-26 37920 (615) 544-9625

Memphis: Mid-South Eye Bank for Sight Restoration, 188 South Bellevue, #125, P.O. Box 40627 38104 (901) 726-8267

Nashville: Lions Eye Bank of Middle Tennessee, Inc., 101 Medical Arts Building, 1211 21st Ave. S. 37212 (615) 320-0620

TEXAS: *Abilene:* District 2-E1 Lions Eye Bank, Inc., First State Plaza East, Suite 150 79602 (915) 673-7334

Amarillo: Lions Hi-Plains Eye Bank of District 2-T1, Inc., High Plains Baptist Hospital — 5th Floor, 1600 Wallace Blvd. 79106 (806) 359-5101 (24 hours)

Austin: Lions Eye Bank of District 2-S3, Inc., 1201 W. 38th 78705 (512) 454-3937

Corpus Christi: Lions Eye Bank of South Texas, Inc., Box 7343 78415 (512) 881-4788 (24 hours)

Dallas: Lions Sight and Tissue Foundation, University of Texas Health Science Center, 401 Forensic Science Building, 5323 Harry Hines Blvd. 75235-9074 (214) 688-3908 (24 hours) (800) 433-6667

El Paso: West Texas Lions Eye Bank, 1101 North Stanton, Suite 807 79902 (915) 532-6044

Fort Worth: Lions Organ & Eye Bank of District 2-E2, Inc., 1429 St. Louis 76104 (817) 921-2996

Houston: Lions Eyes of Texas Eye Bank, Cullen Eye Institute, 6501 Fannin, Suite C-307 77030 (713) 798-5500

Galveston: Lions Eyes of Texas Eye Bank, Dept. of Ophthalmology, UTMB, Room #323, Clinical Science Building 77550 (409) 763-1160

Lackland AFB: Central USAF Eye Bank, Dept. of Ophthalmology, SGHSE, Wilford Hall USAF Medical Ctr. 78236-5300 (512) 670-6583

Lubbock: District 2-T2 Great Plains Lions Eye Bank, P.O. Box 5901 79417 (806) 762-2242

McAllen: Lions Eye Bank of South Texas, Inc., Valley Satellite Office, P.O. Box 4443 78502-4443 (512) 632-4945

Port Arthur: Lions Eyes of Texas Eye Bank, 3600 Gates Blvd. 77642 (409) 722-5631

San Antonio: Eye Bank at Baptist Medical Center, 111 Dallas 78286 (512) 222-8431 X3510

Temple: Central Texas Lions Eye Bank, 2401 South 31 Street, Scott & White Eye Department 76508 (817) 774-2297/beeper 1769

Tyler: Life Bank of East Texas, Medical Center Hospital, 1000 Beckham, P.O. Drawer 6400 75711 (214) 531-8816

UTAH: *Salt Lake City:* Utah Lions Eye & Tissue Bank, University of Utah Medical Center, 50 North Medical Drive 84132 (801) 581-2039

VIRGINIA: *Alexandria:* Old Dominion Eye Bank and Virginia Tissue Bank, 4320 Seminary Road 22304 (703) 751-8229

Charlottesville: Old Dominion Eye Bank, P.O. Box 3067 22901 (804) 971-3937

Norfolk: Lions Medical Eye Bank & Hearing Research Center of Eastern Virginia, Inc., Sentara Norfolk General Hospital, 600 Gresham Drive 23507 (804) 628-EYES

Richmond: Old Dominion Eye Bank, Richmond Eye & Ear Hospital, 1001 East Marshall St. 23219 (804) 644-6332

Roanoke: Lions Eye Bank & Research Foundation of Virginia, Inc., 5th & Elm Streets, SW (24016), P.O. Box 1772 24008 (703) 345-8823

WASHINGTON: *Seattle:* Lions Eye Bank of Washington & Northern Idaho, University of Washington, Dept. of Ophthalmology — RC80 98195 (206) 548-4171 (Day)/548-6190 (Nights & weekends)

Spokane: Lions Eye Bank, S 427 Bernard 99204 (509) 458-4907 (24 hours)

WEST VIRGINIA: *South Charleston:* Medical Eye Bank of West Virginia-TBI, 701 Jefferson Rd. 25309 (304) 744-7686

WISCONSIN: *Madison:* Wisconsin Eye Bank — Madison, 600 Highland Avenue 53792 (608) 263-6223

Milwaukee: Wisc. Lions Eye Bank, Medical College of Wisconsin, Milwaukee County Medical Complex, 8700 West Wisconsin Avenue 53226 (414) 257-5543

The Bequeathal of Bodies to Schools of Medicine and Dentistry

The Need for Donations. Bequeathals are increasing, but not fast enough. Also, greater sharing is needed between areas of surplus and shortage. The degree of need in any medical school is likely to change from time to time. It is wise, therefore, to check with nearby medical schools in advance and, if possible, to file bequeathal papers with the medical school before death occurs. Donors with papers on file will take precedence over persons who have not filed in advance. If you wish the ashes returned, check this matter with the medical school. Most, but not all, are glad to do this.

Alternative Plans. It is important to have an alternative plan, preferably through a memorial society, in case a body is not accepted by a medical school. Some schools are amply supplied or may decline a bequeathal because of the condition of the body. A body may be rejected if it is mutilated or autopsied, or if organs other than eyes have been removed. Likewise, contagious diseases, systemic infections, obesity and other medical conditions *may* disqualify a body for medical school use. Check with your local medical school, as schools vary in their requirements and change from time to time.

Procedures at Time of Death. If bequeathal papers are on file, call the school(s) to make arrangements. If papers have not been filed, consult the directory of medical schools following this section and call the nearest school which accepts bequeathals. If the body is accepted, it may be removed immediately to the school if there is to be no service in the presence of the body, as when a memorial service is held instead of a funeral service.

If the body is to be held for viewing or a service, or sent by common carrier, the funeral director should consult the medical school for instructions. If embalming is done, special procedures must be used, as ordinary embalming will disqualify a body for medical school.

Transportation of the Remains. The body may be delivered in a private vehicle, or by a funeral director. If no funeral director is used, someone else must handle the legal papers. In warm weather, the body should be taken to the school within 24 hours, unless refrigeration (which can be by dry ice) or embalming is used. If the body is to be delivered by common carrier it must be prepared by a funeral director. Some medical schools pay no transportation expenses. Most pay the expense within the state or within a certain radius. See the Medical School Directory. Expenses beyond that distance are paid by the family. Incidentally, Amtrak offers fast, cheap service to some 300 points.

A Deeply Meaningful Experience. The family may prefer to take the body to the medical school themselves, using a station wagon. This has been the

UNIFORM DONOR CARD

OF_____
Print or type name of donor
In the hope that I may help others, I hereby make this anatomical gift, if medically acceptable, to take effect upon my death. The words and marks below indicate my desires.

I give: (a) _____ any needed organs or parts
           (b) _____ only the following organs or parts

_____
Specify the organ(s) or part(s)
for the purposes of transplantation, therapy, medical research or education;
           (c) _____ my body for anatomical study if needed.

Limitations or
special wishes, if any:_____

Signed by the donor and the following two witnesses in the presence of each other:

_____   _____
Signature of Donor   Date of Birth of Donor

_____   _____
Date Signed   City & State

_____   _____
Witness   Witness

This is a legal document under the Uniform Anatomical Gift Act or similar laws.

practice in our family, and we would not think of turning it over to someone else. It is something we can do for the loved one and helps us to accept the loss. The body may be placed in a box or on a stretcher or a plain canvas cot, or simply wrapped in a blanket. People are repelled by death and often shrink from handling a dead body. In practice, however, the privilege of helping to care for the body of a friend or a loved one is a deeply meaningful experience. Too often in modern life we withdraw from reality or call in a professional to do things we might benefit by doing for ourselves.

Legal Papers.   While the legal procedures in our state are simple, this varies from state to state. See Chapter 5, "Simple Burial and Cremation," Transporting of Bodies, page 59.

Message to Recipients.   I am attaching the following message to my bequeathal form and related documents, to be delivered to the students who will be making use of my body, subject to the approval of the Dean of the Anatomy Department and signed only "The Donor:"

> I am pleased that my body may, after my death, be of service to humankind in the training of doctors. This opportunity adds a creative dimension to my death and I appreciate your helping to make it possible.   — The Donor

Medical Schools of Canada and the U.S.

This information was compiled with the help of the schools of medicine, dentistry and osteopathy in the United States, Canada and Puerto Rico. It includes the degree of need of each school for the bequeathal of bodies and the distance, if any, from which the school will pay transportation. The list is in geo-alphabetical sequence.

Medical School Directory

Key to this directory:

DEGREE OF NEED	TRANSPORTATION PAID
U- Urgent Need	W/S- Within State
M- Moderate Need	W/P- Within Province
A- Supplies ample	150 mi- Within that radius
N- No bequeathals	Local- Local area only
needed	None- No transportation paid

Canadian Medical Schools

U. of Calgary, Faculty of Medicine, 3330 Hospital Dr. NW, Calgary AB T2N 4N1
(403)220-6950 U $125

U. of Alberta, Faculty of Med., Edmonton AB T6G 2H7
(403)492-3355 U W/P but not local

U. of B.C., Faculty of Med., Vancouver BC V6T 1W5
(604)228-2498 A Local

U. of Manitoba, Anatomy Dept., 730 William Ave., Winnipeg MAN R3E 0W3
(204)788-6652 M $50

Memorial U., Faculty of Med., Prince Philip Drive, St.John's NFLD A1B 3V6
(709)737-6727 U W/P

Dalhousie U., Faculty of Med., Tupper Medical Bldg., Halifax N.S. B3H 4H7
(902)494-2051 A W/P (Mar.)

158   Appendix 8 / ANATOMICAL GIFTS

McMaster U., Dept. of Anatomy, 1200 Main St. W., Hamilton **ONT** L8N 3Z5 (416)525-9140 M Local

Queen's U., Faculty of Med., Dept. of Anatomy, Kingston **ONT** K7L 3N6 (613)545-2600 M W/P $120

U. of Western Ontario, Faculty of Medicine, Dept. of Anatomy, Richmond St., London **ONT** N6A 5C1 (519)661-3014/2075 M None

U. of Ottawa, Anatomy Dept., Hlth. Sci. Ctr, 451 Smyth Rd., Ottawa **ONT** K1H 8M5 (613) 737-6613/6504 M None

U. of Toronto, Anatomy Dept., Med. Sciences Bldg., Toronto **ONT** M5S 1A8 (416)978-2692 M None

McGill U., Dept. of Anatomy, 3640 Univ. St., Montreal **P.Q.** H3A 2B2 (514)398-6335 M Local

U. de Montreal, Dept. of Anatomy, Pavillon principal R-816, 2900 Boul. Edouard-Montpetit, C.P. 6128 Succ. "A", Montreal **P.Q.** H3C 3J7 (514)343-6288 M 100 mi

U. de Sherbrooke, Fac. de Medecine, Departement D'Anatomie, Sherbrooke **P.Q.** J1H 5N4 (819)563-5555/564-5271 A Local

Univ. of Saskatchewan, College of Medicine, Dept. of Anat., Saskatoon **SASK** S7N 0W0 (306)966-4075 M W/P

U.S. Medical Schools

Anatomy Board of Puerto Rico, Med. Sci. Bldg., 5th Fl. #503, San Juan **P.R.** 00936 (800)758-2525×1510 U W/PR

U. of Alabama, Dept. of Cell Biology & Anatomy, UAB Station, Birmingham **AL** 35294 (205)934-4494 M Local

U. of So. Alabama, Structural & Cellular Biol., 2042 Med. Sciences Bldg., Mobile **AL** 36688 (205)460-6490 M None

U. of Arizona, Coll. of Med., Anat. Dept., Tucson **AZ** 85724 (602)626-6084 M Local

U. of Arkansas, Coll. of Med., Anatomy Dept., Little Rock **AR** 72205 (501)686-5180 A W/S

U.C. at Davis, School of Med., Dept. of Human Anatomy, Davis **CA** 95616 (916)752-2100 M 30 mi

U.C. at Irvine, Dept. of Anatomy & Neurobiology, College of Med., Irvine **CA** 92717 (213)856-6061 M Local

U.C. at San Diego, Sch. of Med., Learning Resources Office, La Jolla **CA** 92093 (619)534-4536 U W/C

Loma Linda U., Anatomy Dept., Loma Linda **CA** 92350 (714)824-4301 M None

U.C. at L.A., Dept. of Anatomy & Cell Biology, School of Med., Los Angeles **CA** 90024 (213)825-9563 M 50 mi

U. of So. Calif. School of Med., 1333 San Pablo St. Los Angeles **CA** 90033 (213)222-0231/225-7825 M 50 mi

Coll. of Osteopathic Med. of the Pacific, College Plaza, Pomona **CA** 91766-1889 (213)623-6116 M 75 mi

Calif. State Polytechnic Univ., 3801 West Temple Ave., Pomona **CA** 91768 (213)869-4038 N 50 mi

U.of C. at S.F., Sch. of Med., Anatomy Dept., San Francisco **CA** 94143-0902 (818)476-1981 M None

Div. of Human Anat., Stanford U. Med. School, Stanford **CA** 94305-5065 (415)723-2404 M 50 mi

U. of Colorado, School of Med., 4200 E. 9th Ave., B-111, Denver **CO** 80262 (303)270-8554/399-1211 M Local

U. of Conn. Health Ctr., Farmington Ave., Farmington **CT** 06032 (203)223-4340 U W/S

Yale U. School of Medicine, Dept. of Surgery, Sec. of Gross Anatomy, 333 Cedar St., P.O. Box 3333, New Haven **CT** 06510 (203)785-2813 U W/S

Georgetown U. Medical Ctr., Dept. of Anatomy, 3900 Reservoir Rd NW, Washington **D.C.** 20007 (202)687-1157 M 25 mi

Howard U., College of Med., Dept. of Anatomy, Washington **D.C.** 20059
(202)636-6555 A Local

Geo. Washington U., Anat. Dept., 2300 I St. NW, Washington **D.C.** 20037
(202)994-3511 U W/S

Anatomical Bd. of Fla., U. of Fla., Coll. of Med., Gainesville **FL** 32610   (205)392-3588/800628-2594(in FL) M None

U. of Miami, School of Med., Dept. of Cell Biology & Anatomy, P.O.Box 016960, Miami **FL** 33101
(305)547-6691 M None

Anat. Dept., Coll. of Med., U. of S. FL, 12901 Bruce B. Downs Blvd., Tampa **FL** 33612   (813)974-2843 A None

Emory U. School of Med., Dept. of Anatomy & Cell Biology, Atlanta **GA** 30322   (404)727-6242 M 50 mi

Morehouse School of Medicine, 720 Westview Dr., SW, Atlanta **GA** 30310
(404)752-1560/1500 M 50 mi

Med. Coll. of Ga., School of Med., Anatomy Dept., 1120 15th St., Augusta **GA** 30912   (404)721-3731 M W/S

Mercer U. School of Med., 1550 College St., Macon **GA** 31207
(912)752-2700/2555 A 70 mi

U. of Hawaii, Dept. of Anatomy & Repro. Biol., 1960 East-West Rd., Honolulu **HI** 96822
(808)948-7131 A Local

Anatomical Gift Assn. of Ill., 2240 W. Fillmore, Chicago **IL** 60612
(312)733-5283 U None

Indiana Univ., Anatomical Educ. Program, Rm. 258, Med. Sc. Bldg., 635 Barnhill Dr, Indianapolis **IN** 46223
(317)274-7450 M None

Univ. of Osteopathic Med. & Health Sci., 3200 Grand Ave., Des Moines **IA** 50312   (515)271-1400 M W/S

U. of Iowa, Coll. of Med., Dept. of Anatomy, Iowa City **IA** 152242
(319)335-7762 A None

U. of Kansas Med. Ctr., Dept. of Anatomy & Cell Biology, 39th & Rainbow Blvd., Kan. City **KS** 66103
(913)588-7000 M None

U. of Kentucky Coll. of Medicine, Lexington **KY** 40536-0084
(606)233-5276/5811 M W/S

U. of Louisville Sch. of Med., Health Sciences Center, Louisville **KY** 40292
(502)588-5165 M 50 mi

Bureau of Anatomical Svcs., Dept. of Anatomy, 1901 Perdido St., New Orleans **LA** 70112-1393 (504)568-4012/588-5255
A W/S & MS coast

U. of New England, Coll. of Osteopathic Med., 11 Hills Beach Rd., Biddeford **ME** 04005   (207)283-0171 M W/S

State Anat. Bd., 655 W. Baltimore, Rm. B-026 Baltimore **MD** 21201
(301)547-1222 M W/S

Uniformed Services, U. of the Health Sciences, 4301 Jones Bridge Road, Bethesda **MD** 20814-4799
(301)295-3333 U 150 mi

U. Mass. Med. Sch., Anat.Gift Program, 55 Lake Ave. N., Worcester **MA** 01605
(508)856-2460 M W/S

U. of Mich. Med. Sch., 3626 Med. Science II, Ann Arbor **MI** 48109
(313)764-4359 U None

Wayne State U. Sch. of Med., Anatomy Dept. 540 E. Canfield, Detroit **MI** 48201
(313)577-1188/1198 M Local

Mich. State U., Anatomy Dept. E. Lansing **MI** 48824
(517)353-5398/355-1855 A Local

U. of Minn. Coll. of Med. Sc., Anatomy Bequest Program, 4-135 Jackson Hall, 321 Church St., Minneapolis **MN** 55455
(612)625-1111 M Local

U. of Miss. Medical Center, 2500 N. State St., Jackson **MS** 39216
(601)984-1000 M 300 mi

In Missouri, make bequeathals to individual schools, or to:
Missouri State Anatomical Bd., Dept. of Anatomy & Neurology, School of Med., U. of MO, Columbia **MO** 65212
(314)882-2288 M None

Anatomical Bd. of Nebraska, 42nd & Dewey Aves., Omaha **NE** 68105
(402)559-6249 A W/S

Dept. of Anatomy, U. of Nev., Sch. of Med., Reno NV 89557-0046
(702)784-6113 A Local

Dartmouth Med. Sch., Anat. Dept., Hanover NH 03756
(603)646-7636/7640 M W/S & VT

U. of Med. and Dentistry of NJ, NJ Med. Sch., 185 S. Orange Ave. Newark NJ 07103   (201)456-4648 M W/S

UMDNJ, School of Osteopathic Medicine, 40 Laurel Rd., Stratford NJ 08084
(604)346-7050 A W/S

UMDNJ-Robert Wood Johnson Med. Sch., Anatomical Assn., 675 Hoes Lane, Psacataway NJ 08854
(908)463-4580/4586 M W/S

Univ. of N.M., Anatomy Dept., North Campus, Albuquerque NM 87131
(505)277-2555 M W/S

Anat. Gift Prog., Dept. of Anat., Albany Medical College, 47 New Scotland Ave, Albany NY 12208
(518)445-5379 M 120 mi

State U. of N.Y., Health Sc. Ctr at Brooklyn, William T. West, Ph.D., Dir. of Donor Prog., Box 5, 450 Clarkson Ave., Brooklyn NY 11203
(212) 270-1014/2379 U 100 mi

State U. of NY at Buffalo, Sch. of Med., Anat. Sciences Dept., Attn. Dr. R. Dannenhoffer, 313 Farber Hall, Buffalo NY 14214   (716)831-2912 M 100 mi

Columbia U. Coll. of Physicians & Surgeons, 630 W. 168th St., New York NY 10032   (212)305-3451 U 100 mi

Cornell U. Med. Coll., 1300 York Ave., New York NY 10021
(212)746-6140 U 90 mi

Mt. Sinai Med. Ctr., One Gustave L. Levy Pl., N.Y. NY 10029
(212)241-7057 M 150 mi

N.Y. Univ., Dept. of Cellular Biology, Anatomy Dept. Attn. Dr. Bogart, 550 First Ave., N.Y. NY 10016
(212)340-5378 U 50 mi

Yeshiva U., Albert Einstein Coll. of Med., Eastchester Rd & Morris Park Ave., New York. NY 10461
(212)430-3142 U Local

U. of Rochester Sch. of Med., Anat. Gift Prog., 601 Elmwood Ave., Rochester NY 14642
(716)275-2592/2272 (evenings, etc.)
M Local

Dept. of Anat. Sciences, Sch. of Med., Health Sci. Ctr., SUNY at Stony Brook, Stony Brook NY 11794
(516)444-3111 U 100 mi

State U of NY Health Sc. Ctr.-Syracuse, Dept. of Anat & Cell Biol., 766 Irving Ave., Syracuse NY 13210
(315)464-5120 U W/S

N.Y. Med. Coll., Basic Sc. Bldg.,Valhalla NY 10595
(914)993-4025/4226 U 100 mi

U of NC, Medical Sciences Teaching Lab, Attn: M. Phelps, Chapel Hill NC 27514   (919)966-1134 M-U if needed

Duke Med. Center, Anatomy Dept., Box 3170, Durham NC 27710
(919)684-4124 M None

E. Carolina U., Sch. of Med., Greenville NC 27858-4354
(919)551-2849 A W/S

Bowman Gray Sch. of Med., Winston-Salem NC 27103
(919)748-4368 A None

U. of North Dakota Sch. of Med., Anatomy Dept., Grand Forks ND 58202
(701)777-2101 M W/S

Ohio U. Coll. of Osteopathic, Med., Rm.#135, Grosvenor Hall, Athens OH 45701-2979
(614)593-1800/594-2416 U W/S

U. of Cincinnati Coll. of Med., Cincinnati OH 45267-0521
(513)558-5612 M None

Case Western Reserve Med. Sch. 2109 Adelbert Rd., Cleveland OH 44106
(215)368-3430/221-9330 M 75 mi

Ohio State U., Anatomy Dept. 333 W. 10th Ave., Columbus OH 43210
(614)292-4831 A $1/mi W/S $50 min.

Wright State U., Sch. of Med., Donated Body Prog., Anat. Dept., Dayton OH 45435   (513)873-3066 A Local

NE Ohio Univ. Coll. of Med., Rootstown OH 44272 (216)325-2511×255 U 75 mi

Med. Coll. of Ohio at Toledo, P.O. 10008, 3000 Arlington Ave., Toledo OH 43699-0008   (419)381-4172 M None

U. of Okla. Health Sci. Ctr, Box 26901, Rm 100-BSEB, Attn. Pam Lawson, Okla. City OK 73190   (405)271-2424 M W/S

Coll. of Osteopathic Med. of Okla. State Univ., 1111 W. 17th St., Tulsa OK 74107   (918)582-1972 M W/S

Oregon Hlth. Sci. Univ., Sch. of Med., Anatomy Dept., Portland OR   97201
(503)494-8302/7811 M None

Humanity Gifts Registry of Pa., 130 S. 9th St., #1550, Philadelphia PA   19107
(215)922-4440 U W/S $50

Brown Univ., Box-G, Div. of Biology & Medicine, Providence RI   02912
(401)863-3355/1000 M W/S

Medical University of S.C., Dept. of Anatomy & Cell Biology, Dr. Donald R. DiBona, 171 Ashley Ave., Charleston SC 29425   (803)792-3521 M W/S

Univ. of S.D. School of Medicine, Vermillion SD 57069
(605)677-5321/624-3932 U 150 mi

E. TN State U., James H. Quillen Coll. of Med., Anat. Dept., Box 19,960A, Johnson City TN   37614
(615)929-6241 A 150 mi

U. of TN Ctr. for Health Sci. 875 Monroe Ave., Memphis TN   38163
(901)528-5965 (bus. hrs.)
(901)528-5500(24 hrs.) U W/S*

Meharry Med. Coll., 1005 Todd Blvd., Nashville TN   37208
(615)327-6308/254-9418 U 200 mi

Vanderbilt Univ. Sch. of Med., Vanderbilt Anat. Donation Prog., 203 Light Hall, Nashville TN   37232
(615)322-7948 A 50 mi

TX A&M U. Med. Coll., Anat. Dept., College Station TX   77843
(409)845-4913/822-1571 M 250 mi

Baylor Coll. of Dent. Anat. Dept., 3302 Gaston Ave., Dallas TX   75246
(214)828-8270/8290 A 200 mi

U. of Tex. Southwestern Medical Center at Dallas, Div. of Anatomy, 5323 Harry Hines Blvd., Dallas TX   75235-9039
(214)688-2221/2232 M 50 mi

Texas Coll. of Osteopathic Medicine Dept. of Anat. & Cell Biology, 3500 Camp Bowie Blvd., Ft. Worth TX 76107-2690   (817)735-2045 U 50 mi

Willed Body Program, U. of Tex., Medical Branch, Rt. H-3, Galveston TX 77550   (409)761-1293 M 300 mi

Baylor Coll. of Med., 1 Baylor Plaza, Houston TX 77030
(713)798-4930 A 100 mi

U. of Tex. Health Sci. Ctr. at Houston, P.O. Box 20708, Houston TX   77225
(713)792-5703 A 250 mi

Texas Tech. U. Health Sc. Ctr., Anatomy Dept., Lubbock TX   79430
(806)743-2700/3111 A 360 mi

U. of Tex. Health Sci. Ctr., 7703 Floyd Curl Dr., San Antonio TX 78284-7762
(512)567-3900 A 100 mi

U. of Utah, Sch. of Med., Anat. Dept., Salt Lake City UT   84132
(801)581-6728/2121 M 50 mi

U. of Vt., Coll. of Med., Dept. of Anat. & Neurobio., Burlington VT   05405
(802)656-2230/3131 M None

E. VA. Med. School, Anat. Dept., Box 1980, Norfolk VA   23501
(804)446-5640/786-2479 A W/S

State Anatomical Div., Dept of Health, Richmond VA   23219
(804)786-2479/3174 A W/S

U. of Wash. Dept. of Biological Structure, SM-20, Sch. of Med., Seattle WA 98195   (206)543-1860 M Local

Marshall U. School of Med., Huntington WV 25755-9350 (304)696-7382 A W/S

---

*Pay expenses for preliminary embalming and transportation within the state, provided donor has filed a bequest with us prior to death. Accept donations initiated by the next-of-kin following death only when expenses are prepaid by the estate. For next-of-kin gifts, the payment requirement is waived if death occurs in the local area (Shelby County).

W. Va. Sch. of Osteopathic Med., Human Gift Registry, 400 N. Lee St., Lewisburg WV 24901
(304)645-6270 M W/S

W. Va. Univ., Human Gift Registry, Morgantown WV 26506
(304)293-6322 A W/S

U. of Wisc. Med. Sch., Anat. Dept., 325 SMI, Madison WI 53706
(608)262-2888 M W/S

The Med. Coll. of Wisc., Dept. of Anat. & Cellular Biol., Attn: Dr. S. Kaplan, 8701 Watertown Plank Rd., Milwaukee WI 53226 (414)257-8261/8262 M None

REFERENCE

[1]Canadian statistics are from the Health Services and Promotion Branch, Health and Welfare Canada, Ottawa, Ontario K1A 1B4. U.S. figures are from the United Network for Organ Sharing.

INDEX

Acceptance of death, *xv*, 10, 12, 18

Acquired immunodeficiency syndrome (AIDS): *ix*, 16-17, 20; in blood donors, 149; in organ donors, 84; special problems of survivors, 28. *See also* AIDS patients.

Alzheimer's Disease, *ix;* 13, 14, 16, 99; need for donated tissues of, 84

Alzheimer's Disease and Related Disorders Association, Inc., 16, 99

AIDS. *See* Acquired immunodeficiency syndrome.

AIDS patients: discrimination against, 17, 49; family relationships of, 17; home care of, 16-17; problems of, 28; resources for, 17, 20, 99; support groups for, 99; treatment by funeral directors, 49

American Association of Retired Persons, 56

American Funeral, The, (Bowman), 2, 71, 99

American Medical Association, views on right to die, 36

American Red Cross, Blood Services Laboratories, 149

American Way of Death, The, (Mitford), *ix-x,* 2, 47, 71, 97

Americans Against Human Suffering, 42, 99

Anatomical gifts. *See* Transplantation of organs and tissues.

Anatomical Gifts Act, (U.S.), 86

Anger: in bereaved children, 26; in the bereaved, 22; in the terminally ill, 12

Arthur Morgan School, *xi*, 10, 39, 60

Artificial feeding in terminal illness: in home care, 15; right to refuse, 35; under state living will laws, 35

Ashes. *See* Cremated remains.

Association for Death Education and Counseling, 3, 99

Autopsy, effect on body disposition, 86

Baty, Ann, 71, 127

Bequeathal. *See* Body bequeathal.

Bereavement: 6; after a death from AIDS, 28; educational materials on, 93; grieving process in, 21-22; growth through, 21, 27, 31; importance of physical care in, 30; in children, 26; in refugees, 30; of parents, 26-27; overload of, 31; personal experiences of, 22-25, 30; professional help in resolving, 29; support groups in, 24-25, 29, 99-102; use of tranquilizers in, 30. *See also* Anger; Grief; Guilt.

Bibliography, 91-97

Blood, donation of, 149-150

Body bequeathal: 85, 155-162; necessity for alternative plans in, 155; legal papers needed for, 157; message to recipients, 157; need for, 155; procedures for, 53, 156; transportation in, 156

Body disposition: after organ donation, 85; alternatives for, 49-50; by donation to medical school, *xii*, 49-50, 53; family participation in, 50, 156-157; legal authority for, 157; planning for, 51-52, 156-157. *See also* Body bequeathal; Caskets; Organs and tissues.

Books and periodicals, 91

Bowman, LeRoy, 2, 71, 97

Burial: 7, 50-51; by family, 23, 60. *See also* Cemeteries; Committal services; Funerals; Memorial Services; Transportation; Grave.

Burial boxes, homemade and other, 111-113. *See also* Caskets.